R.D. Laing and Me: Lessons in Love

by

Roberta Russell

with

R.D. Laing

Designer: Harold Krieger
Typeface: Zapf Humanist
Printer: BookCrafters
Technical Consultants: Maureen & William A. Hopkins
Cover photograph of R.D. Laing by Roberta Russell

We gratefully acknowledge permission to use material from the following sources: The Scottish National Portrait Gallery, Portrait of R.D. Laing by Victoria Crowe; Pantheon Books, a division of Random House, Inc., selections from *Sonnets*, copyright 1979, by R.D. Laing; Penguin Books Ltd., *The Politics of Experience*, by R.D. Laing, (Penguin Books, 1967) copyright R.D. Laing, 1962; *1990 Britannica Book of the Year*, copyright 1990 by Encyclopaedia Britannica, Inc., and from Ann Laing, Karen Laing Heenan, Lida Moser, Matthew J. Reynolds, Leon Redler, M.D. and David Dempsey for photographs and the permission to use them.

Dedication

Dedicated to the courageous who are willing to devote their finest level of attention and intelligence to the adventure of loving another human being.

"Whatsoever thy hand findeth to do, do it with thy might; for there is no work, nor device, nor knowledge, nor wisdom, in the grave, whither thou goest."

Ecclesiastes 9:10

Guided by the research-supported belief that empathy between a client and therapist is the active agent in therapeutic change, and motivated by my desire to help R.D. Laing increase his income and thereby become part of his life, in 1981 I suggested to Laing that he write a book telling his readers how to have a therapeutic relationship with a carefully selected person outside the confines of therapy. He immediately countered with the proposition that I join him in London to write such a book, and by doing so, we could try out this sort of constructive relationship ourselves. Our purpose was to create a successful "how-to" book and to increase our personal options as one does in a successful therapy. That is the way this book—which is actually a true love story—began.

Table of Contents

Chapters

Contraindications

by

R.D. Laing, M.D.

This book is about power and love. It is intended to give you, our reader, the power to get what you love. The power which this book may confer on you works only when you love the power of love, when you are in love with love and not with power.

A life-denier, a living liar, will only do himself further in by trying to use the truth to better disguise his or her lies.

So one's heart has got to be in the right place, or one will inevitably get the wrong end of the stick. Nothing you can do anyway (we hope you are that smart), in trying out any of the mental magic of discipline prescribed in the following pages, will possibly do anyone else but <u>you</u> harm. It will only turn against you, if, whatever you do, you prefer power to love.

Acknowledgements

I am grateful to Daphne Merkin for her creative suggestions and empathic connection; to Francis Mechner, Ph.D. for his liberating insights; to Professor Howard Latin for his critical scrutiny; Robert E. Gould M.D., Michael Brod and Robert Hajdu, Ph.D., J.D. for their structural recommendations; to Professors Fred Supnick, and Moshe Dror, Ph.D.; to Janet Spencer King, Sara Sklaroff, Claire Doyle, Audrey D. Melkin, Richard Stevens Condon, Bella Besson, Matthew J. Reynolds, and to the distinguished members of the psychotherapeutic community cited here for their generous input: to Suzanne L. Weissman, Ph.D., Selma Lewis, Ph.D., M. Barry Flint and Virginia Brooke Flint for their astute feedback; to Werner Engel, M.D. for his numinous contributions and to Arnold Bernstein, Ph.D. who both connected me to the beauty of psychoanalytic thought and provided editorial suggestions. I am particularly indebted to Joseph S. Murphy, Ph.D., Chancellor of The City University of New York, both for his generosity in making available the resources of the libraries affiliated with the University and for his sagacious and penetrating feedback. I am thankful for the unstinting technical support from Tom Atwood, William C. Sabo and Janosh Szebedinszky and for the encouragement of my friends who offered their attention and feedback throughout this endeavor. I especially wish to thank Suzanne Smith whose careful editing and generosity of spirit ultimately carried this endeavor to fruition.

Most of all, I appreciate Harold Krieger for his loving support, sensitive observations and many attentive readings of this work.

THE DEAL: Psychotherapy Between Friends

"Existence...finds its validation when across the gulf of our idioms and styles, our mistakes, errings and perversities, we find in the other's communication an experience of relationship established, lost, destroyed or regained. We hope to share the experience of a relationship, but the only honest beginning, or even end may be to share the experience of its absence."

"The psychotherapeutic relationship is therefore a re-search. A search constantly reasserted and reconstituted, for what we have all lost and whose loss some can perhaps endure a little more easily than others, as some people can stand lack of oxygen better than others, and this re-search is validated by the shared experience of experience regained in and through the therapeutic relationship in the here and now."

R.D. Laing, *The Politics of Experience*

One of the most difficult and dangerous of all human endeavors is the quest to meet another person on common ground, while at the same time recognizing the essential, transcendental inaccessibility of that other. That is the challenge of life and of this book.

This tale is a slice of life which occurred between R.D. Laing and me. My attempt to use the power of love to increase my options became our endeavor to record our unfolding friendship and turn it to account. As if on cue, our relationship evolved in the form of a classic psychoanalytical model of resistance and transference into transformation and resolution.

This is a story of power and love, the power to get what you love, what you dream. We all dream, but I, who know detachment—having lost my immediate family, father, mother and brother, between my twenty-fifth and thirty-third year, and having had my husband of seven years cleaved away by then, too—*I live my dreams.*

And what do my dreams have to do with Dr. R.D. Laing? He was made to order:

As an adolescent I wanted to be a great psychoanalyst, saving distraught heroes of mythical grandeur. Perhaps a result of unresolved Oedipal conflicts? you're thinking. Perhaps—I did adore my father, but that's another story. At 16 I read Freud and imagined scenes of intimate breakthroughs with brilliant, powerful men and me as the sole healing witness—the dreams of youth.

Later on, in adult life I devoted much of my time to the study of human relationships, having sufficiently mastered earning a living as a self-employed headhunter—a recruiter of computer professionals—to limit my work activities to a few hours per week. Through relentless reading, observation and analysis, I followed the trail, like an Indian scout searching for home. A lot of reweaving remained to be done. Picking up where I had left off before all the tumultuous departures of my family, I found that my real occupation had become that of a *heart* hunter, always on the watch for a kindred spirit. In the absence of a natural family, I had decided to create an intentional one. You can't go on forever without belonging to someone. As the statistics bear out, isolation will take its toll and kill you.

And so head and heart hunter that I was, I went after my prey. The quarries were the best I could find. Of course, the secret ingredient underpinning all this magic was that the hunter had to love the prey —love them to pieces, in fact.

In 1979, my lifelong quest for an understanding of why people do things was formalized when I was elected to take charge of a fact-finding committee as a public member of NAAP, The National Accreditation Association and American Examining Board of Psychoanalysis, Inc. I was asked to explore the research on "what works in psychotherapy" and make recommendations in the interest of protecting the public, the consumers of psychotherapy.

The purpose of my *Report* was to seek out the common denominator of the "active ingredients" in the therapy process. What I discovered in the literature and in interviews was quite different from what any of the individual schools of thought had postulated, not excluding NAAP. *It does not matter whether one is a behaviorist or a psychoanalyst. Techniques themselves do not cause therapeutic change. They are only a thing to do together, while you are together, perhaps one of many potentially useful "things to do." It is primarily the empathy and intention between the psychotherapist and client that is healing.* The technique used is just incidental to change. Two years later I formalized this verbal report in a book entitled, *Report On Effective Psychotherapy: Legislative Testimony.*

Because the findings were unusually clear and well documented, they were picked up by the National Center for the Study of the Professions in Washington, D.C. In July, 1980 I formally presented the *Report* as an invited guest to the European Association of Humanistic Psychology (EAHP) in Geneva, Switzerland. My conclusions were picked up because they legitimized and therefore empowered the *healing person* regardless of his or her credentials. After my presentation the board of the EAHP invited me to present the *Report* under its aegis to the World Health Organization (WHO) in Geneva. WHO then requested an official alliance with EAHP. From a lone personal quest to learn what makes people grow I had been catapulted to reporting my findings to international professionals and policy-makers. I felt like I was riding the crest of a wave.

Next I was invited to speak at a psychotherapy-outcome congress in Saragosa, Spain, and present the *Report's* findings. The legendary British psychiatrist R.D. Laing was to be the featured speaker.

I had read Laing's *Politics of Experience* and *The Divided Self*. Dazzled by his clarity and brilliance, I was thrilled at the prospect of meeting him.

Why Me?

When I think about it all now, 10 years later, I think that somehow I had known something important would happen to me with Laing even before he proposed that I join him in writing a book. Perhaps it was a premonition? Maybe it was because my access to people seemed to be increasing much faster than I had anticipated.

In any event, having honed myself into the habit of attempting to replace the loss of treasured friends with other significant spirits, I was ready to meet Laing.

Richard Graham, a gifted financial architect and blithe spirit, who was then my most perceptive friend, and the core of my created family, had recently died of cancer, leaving me once again bereft, adrift, alone, and pitched about on a sea of self-doubt. Why was I so consistently abandoned? Was I just unlucky or perhaps unworthy of love?

I ate too much and isolated myself, dwelling perpetually on these disheartening thoughts. I was afraid that a trip to Spain at this turbulent time might upset my already precarious balance. But serendipitously, Arthur Carter, Richard's brilliant business partner, visited me that summer, all tanned and robust-looking, to tie up loose ends. Exercising his particular gift for strategic intervention, he strongly advised me to go to Spain, give my talk, and meet the famous R.D. Laing. He imagined that I would not be lonely for long and he pointed out that I could always come home if I turned out be unhappy after all. As an aside he also reinvested all my savings for me and elusively disappeared from my scene.

Arthur Carter had restored my balance. Now, even in my debilitated state the chance to meet R.D. Laing buoyed me up, and I was filled, however wistfully, with the hope of an inspired communion with this legendary man who tread so gracefully in the mysterious realm of understanding and compassion.

And so in September, 1980 I marshalled my forces and left for Saragosa, Spain. My friend Knut who was also one of the conference organizers exuberantly introduced me to Laing as a woman he was in love with. In this respect I was one of many fortunate women and I don't imagine that Laing took Knut's declarations too seriously.

We were ensconced at a three-week-long conference at the Monasterio de Piedra, a twelfth-century monastery-cum-hotel, situated in the middle of a large natural park, in a picturesque setting of lakes, waterfalls and grottoes. Although I would occasionally pass Laing strolling about in this pleasant environment, he did not seek me out. Even though we had been formally introduced, he would usually just give me a nod and go on his way. After more than a week of general proximity at the psychotherapy conference in Spain, Laing had rarely spoken to me. He seemed devoid of normal salutations in the polite behavior department. So when he finally did talk to me, his comments were framed in stark relief. Everything that he said or did then seemed to be laden with meaning. I was as attuned to his subtle communications as a newborn baby is to her mother's face.

From the beginning, Laing was subtly making himself known to me. At first it was barely apparent.

During my sojourn in Spain, Laing spoke to me only infrequently, but I stayed in his sphere and felt that I had his attention. Without knowing why, I felt peaceful when he was around. Although he didn't have much to do with me then, I nevertheless found myself entranced with him.

Late into the night he played melancholy Cole Porter tunes on the piano in the monastery which housed the conference, as a coterie of his "portable community" milled around the large white-walled room. One night the room was filled with probably 25 or 30 people. I was unable to tell what role they played in their lives outside of this conference—they might have been therapist or patient. No such distinctions were made here. I noticed that the sensitive-looking young man, sitting next to me, with his back against the wall was silently crying. Uncharacteristically I reached over to touch him, but he motioned me away, wanting to be left to his own private thoughts. I looked back toward Laing who was still at the piano undisturbed by the naturalness of those around him.

For most of the evening Laing's wife, Jutta was conspicuously absent, and I assumed that she was with her five year old son, Max, who was also attending the conference. Unlike Laing, Jutta was openly friendly to me. She invited me to join her and her friends for coffee and introduced me to a soulful-looking German man about whom she seemed particularly enthusiastic. She seemed happy with her group of friends, almost glowing.

Later that evening she sporadically made "guest appearances," but her attentions to Laing appeared oddly forced in the smoky atmosphere. She danced with Laing while someone else took a turn at the piano, and he held her with a tentativeness that I had not previously noticed. Laing seemed strangely vulnerable, and time had not withered my save-the-powerful-man fantasy. It was going strong.

Touch Me

In the course of the conference Laing was called upon to arbitrate a serious dispute among the organizers. The silky adroitness of his political skills as he orchestrated the sudden expulsion of a couple of discordant organizers awed and surprised me. Although I was not close to the shunned couple, this strange expulsion scene unexpectedly brought tears to my eyes.

I had always thought of empathy as the basic connective energy of human life, and true to form, I wrote out my ideas and feelings at the time in a notebook:

Laing touched me for the first time with the phrase, "When you cry for others you cry for yourself." He said this to me out of context, some time after he had discreetly seen me shed tears — tears I thought were unobserved — for an ostracized conference organizer whom I barely knew. With this phrase he went straight to my heart and he knew it.

To touch is to empathize, is to feel for, is to reach, is to connect. It is through this meaningful communication between two human beings that the energy for constructive change is transmitted. This positive energy exchange is as enlivening as the feeling of aliena- tion — that we create when we treat others as objects — is deaden- ing. Transcending all psychotherapeutic schools of thought, this is a global principle. Empathy is the language of love. When one feels for others, one enters into a communion with all life.

But More of Our Beginnings...

In spite of Laing's promising insightful comment about my tears, and my elaborate and congenial theories about healing and relationships, there were still no connectors or salutations forthcoming at the Humanistic Psychology Conference in Spain. But Laing had me think- ing. What did he really know about me? Did he think I was crying about my own primal expulsions, or was his comment just a shot in the dark?

By the third week in Spain my energy was waning. I was getting my first cold in five years. Normally I am quite an ebullient spirit, but I found myself lonely and persistently dwelling on my need for a reassuring hug from Knut, the now-present-but-preoccupied former beau. Since this hug was not forthcoming in spite of my requests, I thought it might be prudent to take my leave before I deteriorated further.

That very evening I abruptly announced my decision to return immediately from Saragosa to New York City. In spite of Laing's auspicious bit of attention earlier, there was no sign of any potential follow-up, and my stamina was going fast.

As I said my good-byes at the Spanish conference, Laing played the piano with great abandon—only watching, still no salutations—and with just a knowing nod for a good-bye to me. Even now I wish I could remember what he was playing on the piano as I was leaving, but I was less conscious and more afraid then.

Room in Rome

It was just five weeks before I saw Laing again, this time on a crisp fall day at an Italian Humanistic Psychology Congress in Rome. By then I had read his books — 12 in all. We were among the few English-speaking presenters, and I was to report on the results of my psychotherapy-outcome study and do a self-marketing workshop. The two enterprises weren't entirely unrelated.

I can clearly remember sitting on the steps in the receiving room of the *pensione* where all the presenters were to stay. Scheduled presenters were arriving with their bags and being directed to the rooms which would be their lodgings for the three-day congress of the Italian Association of Humanistic Psychology. They spoke to each other in Italian and I thought about the limitations imposed by my lack of foreign language expertise. Although both my psychology-outcome talk and the self-marketing workshop would have an Italian translator, I wondered if there would be anyone to talk to in English.

Just then, Laing walked in, framed in the sunshine from the open doorway. Oblivious of the crowd, he walked directly up to me and he hugged me. We stayed that way, hugging, holding on to the hug. Somehow the hug transported me, and I froze it like a snapshot in time. The particular masculine smell of him, the unfamiliar solid feel of his body under the soft texture of his knitted white sweater and the firmness of his hold on me were not lost with the passing of time. Sometimes I can still feel the continuity and comfort of that hug. It lasted a long time.

I don't remember now who let go first. Laing had never touched me before and inspired by his unforeseen proximity, I fell into an awkwardly expectant mode.

Still there were no salutations—no verbal connectors forthcoming from him. He talked to me in the purest unspoken voice—somehow like a melody continued from some distant past. I wondered about this and made notes in my notebook:

*Maybe we all bring the past to very powerful relationships? Perhaps this is what the therapists call transference? Transference and healing are not confined to the therapist's office. They go together and are a natural, heightened part of life. **An emotionally charged relationship is an important vehicle for transition, but understanding by itself does not necessarily produce change. Nevertheless, transference is not entirely real. It is the transfer of feelings (positive or negative) which were attached to a significant person in the past to someone in the present. Transference is a powerful emotional shorthand in which qualities of a newer person are embellished to further resemble those of an earlier formative person. This sort of attachment is a paste job from the past, but barring its inaccuracies, transference has impact. It moves you to act.***

That evening Laing called on me at my room and asked if I would like to join him and Jutta in their room for a drink. I was surprised on the one hand because he hadn't invited me to any events before when we were in Spain, and on the other because there were so many contenders for the star's company. I decided to take hope from the hug and be optimistic. He had more of a desire for my presence then. Something had changed. The Laings and I began to know each other better. The three of us became steady companions.

Ronnie (as his friends called him) invited me to join him and Jutta on a ride to the Italian YMCA where the Laings were to do an all-day workshop. I felt that I was serving some emerging purpose as they discussed the forthcoming event. I wasn't sure what it was, but being with Ronnie and Jutta made me feel at home. Perhaps there was something about the roles we took with each other that was vaguely familiar? I had fit in naturally like this before in the family scene from which I had sprung myself back in Floral Park, New York. There, my mother, father, and brother all needed me for something and I was always in demand. They were fun—the Laings, that is. My family of origin had turned out to be another sort of story.

Back at the YMCA workshop, hundreds of Italian-speaking participants awaited Laing's arrival. Posters of the event were plastered across the street fences. Laing walked in first, flanked by Jutta and me; I was proudly clutching an interim version of his manuscript of *The Voice of Experience* under my arm. An Italian translator joined us, and I dropped to the side to watch the show. I had never been attracted to workshops, but this one tempted and intrigued me.

Laing offered to take on all comers in an Indian wrestling match. The translator repeated the challenge through the microphone in Italian, and it echoed through the large gymnasium, reverberating from the high ceilings to the bare wooden floors. I watched amazed as confident, muscle-bound young men strode up to the line to have their shot at knocking down the agile, lithe, 54-year-old father figure. Inevitably the challengers landed with a surprising thud on the floor. I couldn't stop grinning. He was establishing his position of leadership—by action, not through words. He knew how to make the right moves. It didn't take brute strength to win. Everyone could see that. **Let your energy work for you**. The Italian translator was superfluous.

The exercises progressed with the organic order of an evolving family, first defining the roles of men and women and then simulating childbirth. At Laing's direction the men walked around the women in circles, impersonating them, and then the women did the same, showing their interpretation of men. The exaggerated message of their perspectives was brought home to everyone with humor and perfect nonverbal clarity.

Subsequently the Laings organized a dramatic rebirthing experience. Ronnie took me aside and informed me of the rationale he was using; he would select the most agitated person to play the "baby" trying to get through a mock birth canal. "Am I in training for something?" I wondered expectantly.

The most belligerent and aggressive souls who volunteered were selected first and dissolved into screams and tears until they were completely depleted (reborn, perhaps?) as they struggled through a man-made, living, clutching birth canal formed by six participants. One explosive, strapping, young man, a resident patient at the therapeutic center we were visiting, having passed through this simulated "birth process," actually had to be carried away unconscious to recover in the arms of his companions. (This now docile "newborn baby" had impulsively jumped me earlier in the day and thrown me on the floor in a stranglehold. Fortunately one of the few Italian words I knew was "basta," which means enough! And so he let me up unharmed, and I had a chance to show my spirit.) The whole spectacle was incredible and fascinating to me.

That night the Laings invited me to go with them to a party given by their friends from The Living Theater. Jutta seemed to enjoy the festivities and drifted off to talk to some familiar-looking, long-haired international actors.

I stayed close to Laing who was sitting cross-legged on the floor. Judith Malina, a small, very smart, intensely animated woman who was co-founder of The Living Theater, casually asked Ronnie what he had done that day. Smiling, he turned to her and said, "Roberta will tell you." And thus my mission took on definition. I was to report what I saw. Perhaps part of love is the redefinition of oneself through the other person's eyes? He seemed to like the way I saw him, and I loved his enjoyment of my interpretations of him.

When I recounted the series of dramatic events which had unfolded in the workshop, filtered through my sense of wonder at what I had seen, Laing seemed pleasantly surprised. I referred to the workshop as a microcosm of society evolving. He grinned and was quite encouraging. I never went too far for Laing. I never went too far from him. I wanted to be his translator and thereby make his subtle behavior more explicit.

One event that I didn't report to Judith Malina was the exercise in which the participants stood back-to-back with interlocking arms and alternately lifted each other off the floor and over their backs, symbolizing mutual trust and support. As I watched from the side, enthralled, Ronnie came over and lifted me off the ground. I had begun to be hopeful. Maybe he would offer me a real lift? Around Ronnie I felt the thrill of learning, of being useful and of having a sense of purpose, even lightheartedness. His piano music made me want to sing, although I didn't because I was afraid.

My presentation was scheduled for the following day. At this gathering in Rome I was doing one of my Self-Marketing workshops, as well as lecturing on my psychotherapy-outcome *Report.* In the Self-Marketing workshops I had conducted for businesses and colleges, I focused on what was most central to the participants, what one might describe as their calling. I recommended a process of self-sculpture, discarding irrelevancies. This was to be done by a combination of meditation, relaxation, and reality testing. Once that process was underway, the client and I would define a market for the client's relevant skills and then set up a marketing plan. This was often quite an exhilarating journey—trying out one's dreams. In Rome, Laing watched the results of this process with interest when workshop participants came to me afterwards asking for more.

On several occasions Laing invited me to join him and Jutta when they went out or when he did a workshop. He seemed to need me for something now. I had his attention. When I returned to New York City, I left enriched and stimulated by my experiences in Rome. The Laings invited me to call if I was in London. I thought wistfully about casually turning up at their door step, but the idea seemed highly impractical. Instead, I went back to my New York City apartment to face the oncoming winter alone, without any further plans to see Laing.

I did call him months later when he was back in London and I was in New York, requesting that he review my new book. Although this took several calls, he eventually did so, and I was in his debt and still dreaming about him. What made me persist? Was it the memory of the unfamiliar hug? Perhaps it was a phrase I had read in *The Politics of Experience*, something about rediscovering our personal worlds and at first discovering a shambles: "Bodies half-dead; genitals dissociated from heart; heart severed from head; head dissociated from genitals." I was convinced that Laing, having written this, must therefore have his head, heart, and genitals all lined up in the right places. His catchy words turned out to be the breeding ground for endless fantasies.

One day, in the early summer of 1981, I got a call from Knut, the aforementioned German friend of both Laing's and mine. He thought Laing was in real trouble, maybe even suicidal. He said Laing was having marital problems and was not earning as much money as he needed to carry on in the style to which he had grown accustomed. Knut's message was intense and graphic, and instantly my familiar save-the-powerful-man fantasy switched on. Laing was world famous, a charismatic leader, a poet, and a subtle observer of the human condition. I knew he wanted to make money selling books in America. This task didn't seem so difficult to me. As for his marital problems, I had no means to approach him—I had plenty of ideas, but at that time he had not encouraged me in this arena.

With ample food for thought, I wondered: *Why not encourage Laing to popularize the empowering findings of my investigation into the effective ingredients of psychotherapy? He had unraveled these mysteries independently through his own courage and experience and expressed his conclusions indelibly with poetic clarity.*

Could one get curative results if one picked the best person available and formed a useful project or game plan with him or her? If the selected partner and I followed an exemplary, jointly agreed to, and very clear path, would we create a way of being which fostered mutual confidence? The purpose of this approach was to maximize the possibility of increasing trust through increasing trustworthiness. **If good human relationships provide the curative powers to free us from the shackles of loneliness and** *demoralization that underlie much of our destructive and addictive behaviors, why not motivate a fellow traveler to empower us? Healing is, after all, not the exclusive province of psychotherapy, although we can certainly learn something from that model of treatment.*

I reasoned that for most problems, the effectiveness of psychotherapy or lack of it has more to do with the therapist's genuiness, warmth, and regard for her client—the quality of empathy between therapist and client, more than anything else (as perceived by the client, not the therapist).

I had plenty of regard for Laing, and thus, I formulated a plan of action. I would give him the idea of writing a how-to-have-a-relationship book. He was a natural—a dramatic spiritual leader, a medical doctor, a brilliant writer. How could he miss? I thought. Practically everyone who buys how-to books wants to know how to have a better relationship.

It was on the fourth of July in 1981 that I summoned up the courage to call London. I could feel my heart beating as I dialed. Laing listened to my proposal and was intrigued. Wondrously, he suggested that I come to London and do the book with him. He said my visit would be exploratory because *we* didn't know whether we could work together. Before I hung up the phone, I heard the words, "And I love you," come out of my mouth, and then I did not remember hearing a reply.

I hung up the phone leaping into the air. I was no longer alone in the world. I had a sense that now I had the very bond that I was advocating, coupled by the mutually useful thing to do together. Laing gave me what I was looking for, an added piece of myself. I loved him for it. I loved him anyway, just for being alive and being so smart, but now I had a chance to express it. Although I had arranged only a speculative three-day trial with him, I felt as if my entire being had shifted into a different reality. I was flying.

The Preparation

My method with Laing was going to be both heartful and logical. I thought that heart and mind cannot be meaningfully separated, because they are really two aspects of the same force. I imagined that by creating a sanctuary of increased empathy, people would be better able to achieve freedom from the self-made quagmires that prevented them from achieving realistic goals. In line with these ideas, I wanted to achieve two goals that had been persistently difficult for *me*: First I wanted to find a man to love and be loved by with whom I could share my life; and second I wanted to lose thirty-five pounds and be athletically fit. Although I had once before been slim and married to a man I loved, the current realization of both goals had become persistently elusive. I intended the program I was proposing to be an equally fit blueprint for everyone, the whole spectrum of tenacious haunting neurotic excesses: compulsive eating, drinking, smoking, working, isolation, and socializing and sexual behavior.

> "Psychotherapy consists of the paring away of all that stands between us, the props, masks, roles, lies, defenses, anxieties, projections, and introjections, in short all the carryovers from the past, transference and countertransference that we use by habit and collusion wittingly or unwittingly, as our currency for relationships."
>
> R.D. Laing, *The Politics of Experience*

In preparation for my trip to London I went back to my notebook and wrote: *It is not lack of knowing what to do that prevents the wistful but unsuccessful dieter from sticking to an appropriate eating and exercise routine, nor what keeps the deluded and distracted alcoholic from enjoying a more sober and productive life. The most readily available source for mastery of our own good advice must be an empathetic, purposeful relationship with another human being.*

I couldn't imagine a better set and setting to test my theories than meeting with R.D. Laing in Hampstead, England to write a book together. I was riding the crest of a wave once again. There was plenty of time for preparation, though, because it was several months before Laing actually cleared a space for our meeting.

Highly motivated, I continued to read copiously from the annals of psychotherapy literature, and now I also explored various self-help methodologies. Ultimately I submitted myself to the experience of a weekend re-evaluation counseling meeting led by Harvey Jackins, in what looked like an abandoned army camp in Glassboro, New Jersey. There, participants were encourage to take turns emoting. Scheduled emotionality has never been my stock in trade and I stuck it out in the service of learning something that might potentially prove useful in my project with Laing....

It was not until November, 1981 that I actually found myself once again in Laing's presence with the chance to test my mettle.

Home?

"The meeting of two personalities is like the contact of two chemical substances: if there is any reaction, both are transformed."

Carl Jung

One bright day during an early meeting at Laing's house I asked him "What works when psychotherapy is effective?"

"Having a love affair is one of the most therapeutic things you can do," he replied, characteristically skirting the question, while at the same time getting to the heart of the matter and thereby setting the stage for our story. He later explained that *attentiveness is virtually synonymous with therapy*. He said he was acting toward me as he behaved toward someone in therapy with him, and as he treated others in his life as well. I wasn't sure to what extent he meant this, but he had *my* attention. *A fortuitous love affair can open your heart. Emotions surge. The affair creates a stage on which to relive the stultifying emotional traumas of your past, thereby unblocking frozen energy for more refreshing endeavors*. Psychotherapy professionals often refer to this behavior as *"acting out."* I approached our project with pensive optimism.

CHAPTER ONE

The Quest For A Common Metaphor

Love is something far more than the desire for sexual intercourse; it is the principal means of escape from the loneliness which afflicts most men and women throughout the greater part of their lives. There is a deep seated fear in most people of the cold world and the possible cruelty of the herd; there is a longing for affection, which is often concealed by roughness, boorishness or a bullying manner in men, and by nagging and scolding in women. Passionate mutual love while it lasts puts an end to this feeling; it breaks down the hard walls of the ego, producing a new being composed of two in one. Nature did not construct human beings to stand alone, since they cannot fulfill her biological purpose except with the help of another....

Bertrand Russell

In this optimistic state of mind I went to see R.D. Laing in London on November 2, 1981 to write a book with him about how to have a healing relationship, specifically a relationship with a carefully selected partner, while engaging that partner in an appropriately constructive venture. I understood that Laing and I intended to be an example of such a relationship. We wanted to make the book project a financially profitable venture as well. Somehow in the process of trying to find common ground on which to begin our project, Laing asked me to show him how to make more money without any additional effort on his part, perhaps by marketing his books more effectively. Although this seemed somewhat tangential to my purpose in coming to England, it was our starting point.

Thus I found myself bearing a message that Laing did not want to hear. I imagined that Laing had already been well marketed. He was world-famous, and his name opened doors. I intended to tell him that what he had been writing recently didn't serve the potential American readership sufficiently to become best sellers, as some of his earlier books had been. Knowing that he was no exception to the human condition of defensiveness, I was afraid to tell him my thoughts about the root of his money problems.

We had our first meeting at Francis Huxley's house, where Laing had arranged for me to stay. Huxley had given him guest privileges in his nearby flat, and Laing had merely extended them to me. From the airport I took a cab to Huxley's house, and as Laing had instructed, I called him immediately when I arrived there. Jutta answered, sounding unclear about what I should do next, and then R.D. Laing came to the phone.

When I heard his voice on the phone the magic continued; I felt as if I were connected to a direct pipe line to oxygen, and my heart was beating like mad. He arranged to see me a few hours later, after he had completed his last therapy session. Before going out for the afternoon Huxley showed me around the high-ceilinged, five room flat, inviting me to stay in a lovely, peach colored room with abstract oil paintings, fireplace, garden view and shelves of well-read books. Huxley eventually left for two weeks, leaving me alone in the well-stocked flat.

I sat on the couch...and waited. I had never been alone with Laing and was initially anxious at the thought of meeting this great man as a co-author.

Arriving in a black pinstriped suit, complemented by red socks, Laing explained apologetically what he must have considered his unusually formal attire, saying that he had had a meeting with his banker earlier in the day. I thought him absolutely beautiful and harbored the suspicion that he had dressed this way to impress me.

His dark-lashed, hazel eyes peered at me through gold-rimmed spectacles, warm, but wary. I could hear my own breathing. The nearness of him, alone in Francis's apartment, was intense. I imagined his agile wiry legs under his dark trousers. His hair fell softly in shades of gray and brown around his ears and met the darker beard tipped in white which he had grown since our last meeting. The softness of his hair contrasted with the intensity of the strong dark brows, twinkling bright eyes, and sensuous full lips.

We sat down at the well-worn wooden kitchen table, facing each other. Laing lit up a cigarette and leaned back in his chair, one elbow resting on the table as I set up my tape recorder...complete with extending microphone. We began tentatively, and he soon told me that it would take him a while to become illogical, a desirable state from his point of view. Maybe he was anxious, too.

I finally got around to asking him why he was sad. Remember, the original purpose of my mission had been to save him, although I had not shared this secret with Laing. He didn't say he was sad. He didn't say he was not sad. He did say that he was not seeking the sort of cheerfulness that I seemed to exhibit. I noticed that he didn't make much eye contact with me. His eyes were fixed on the cigarette he was rolling (one of many), and his high forehead was shiny where the hair was receding. He didn't want to be my patient or my doctor. He did want to make more money. Over an hour went by, and Huxley returned. "Francis," he said embracingly, his voice warmed by a thick Scottish burr. Laing seemed glad to see him, and we shared some coffee that Francis made by throwing the ground coffee in a regular cooking pot of boiling water. We sweetened it with a brown coarse sugar, set out in an uncovered bowl on the unadorned table, and Laing and Huxley repeated the cigarette ritual. I imagined that they had had similar coffee-cigarette

scenes around this table many times before. Before long a con-
tinuation of our discussion was scheduled for the next day.

When any of us first meet, replete with our organizational constructs, we experience each other as separate creatures, with whom we can communicate enough to pass the sugar or have a drink together at the local bar. For these occasions, polite behavior will suffice. It is polite behavior not to challenge the other person's image of herself or himself. Polite behavior, however, would be inadequate to carry us past the defenses that keep our respective internal organizations intact. Polite behavior was not going to be completely adequate here, if we were to manage to achieve a quantum of intimacy.

I wondered how I could create enough trust while attempting to establish "deeper" communication. How could I create enough trust and motivation to allow for a lowering of Laing's guard, enough to let my way of being in? How could I be really comfortable with him while I still did not feel free to tell him what I had heard of his unhappy marital situation?

I had come to England to co-author a book with Laing which would combine what we had learned about life in a form which we both expected to be useful. I had great expectations, since I saw R.D. Laing both as a spiritual leader and an extremely subtle observer of the human condition, perhaps the best living author I had read on that subject.

When the opportunity presented itself, soon after our first meeting, I took the plunge, suggesting to him that his more-recent books weren't best sellers in America anymore because he was depressed when he wrote them, and because his current concerns were too circumscribed to culminate in bestsellers. As I would quickly learn, he was neither convinced that I was right, nor delighted with my approach.

Laing insisted that his problem was basically financial, the result of inadequate marketing. I knew that he could easily double his earnings by booking more hours as a psychiatrist: He only worked part time at hourly therapy. He explained that he wasn't motivated to work longer hours because he didn't want to spend his time that way. The extra money he could have earned by carrying a full case load really wasn't that important to him. He wanted to earn more money specifically by selling his books — by selling them in America, he said.

I thought that he was very depressed. While betrayal has always been a dominant chord in his work, he now seemed obsessed with it. Now he was honed in on his shaky marital scene. I felt, at the time of our initial encounters, that this distracted him from more expansive issues.

I thought he was not appropriately receptive to new information that conflicted with his early theories: formerly he had treated madness as a journey through which the sufferer may emerge as a more integrated human being. Now he merely stretched the meaning of these earlier concepts and used his brilliance to defend his originally revolutionary theories. Sometimes he seemed to me to be an acrobat walking across a tightrope spread over an abyss — a fame-forged chasm — with only his wits to keep his balance.

He did not address himself to either the reported advances in drug therapies or the dearth of voyagers returning from such passages through madness, now integrated and whole. I thought about it this way: Although Laing's contribution was both profound and far-reaching, this mystical passage through madness was poetic, but probably overrated. I reasoned that Laing was no longer as courageous about new ideas, because he could not bear to look at the truth: the truth was that Laing had fallen for the rewards of fame. He needed adulation like a drug. I also thought that if I blurted all this out to Laing before he grew to love me, I'd be sent back to New York City and written off by him as someone he could not work with. This was the quandary that faced me, sitting there in the heartland of Europe's intellectual aristocracy, surrounded by the books of Francis Huxley and some once belonging to his father, Julian Huxley, that were annotated with margin notes by Konrad Lorenz among others.

I expected to do a form of peer counseling with Laing, sometimes called co-counseling. Having familiarized myself with the counseling approaches of others, I felt that we could customize an approach for ourselves. I knew that Alcoholics Anonymous was among the many self-help groups that incorporate aspects of co-counseling. Reevaluation Counseling, another peer help movement, had attracted large followings primarily through its founder, Harvey Jackins', personal charisma. Here participants followed a structured program to learn to listen to each other sensitively and ventilate their feelings. My brief experience with this process in order to prepare for my endeavor with Laing did not seem to be directly applicable.

On the phone, in the process of organizing our meeting in London, Laing had led me to believe that he was receptive to my suggestion that an unstructured form of co-counseling would be our most effective style; I had a vision of us telling stories together, making eye contact, paring away our defenses, and ultimately, through this bond, gaining the courage to go after our goals. I had a lot to learn. Laing was a master manipulator, and his intimations did not imply forthcoming agreements.

* * *

We were seated in the library in Laing's house, lined with bountifully stocked bookshelves. Throughout the room, books were also neatly stacked on the floor. An elegant Steinway grand was framed by high bay windows. Curiously, Laing's toiletries and smoking materials were kept on the piano, as if the piano top was his bedroom dressing table. As it turned out, it was. Their dog, a Weimaraner called Moon, sat next to me on the couch, eying me suspiciously and growling softly. Laing said that animals can tell when you are afraid. I petted Moon who relaxed in response, snuggling up against me. Laing's apparent awareness of my anxiety was comforting.

Jutta and Max, Laing's six-year-old son, greeted me, and I once again set up my tape recorder on the coffee table. We quickly resumed our discussion of increasing Laing's income, which had begun at our prior meeting at Huxley's flat and gone on from there, while Jutta disappeared into another part of the house and jogging-suit-clad Max quietly hung about curiously examining the microphone.

Laing had claimed that he wasn't being marketed well, but had not expressed interest in altering his commercial value. I took a deep breath and suggested instead the conflicting idea that Laing's creative work was not up to his potential, because he was depressed. The first rule for engendering trust between yourself and another human being is that you have to tell the truth, the whole truth. I therefore could not let go of this topic. I had to speak my mind:

Me	You give me two messages—if you thought you had only a marketing problem, you wouldn't have let me come here and talk about co-counseling. When we talked on the phone you were going to practice co-counseling. You said you were very impressed with it.
RDL	That's what we're doing just now.
Me	All right, this is your version.
RDL	You're addressing yourself a lot to what I think is tangential to what I said was *my* presenting "problem." I am spending more than I am earning.
Me	But you said you don't *have* a presenting problem....
RDL	I said that, having thought about it before you came, and after going into it further last night, I do not have what you call a problem. It's a nuisance. I'm not complaining. I would like as much money to come in as goes out. I hope more money will come in. The way I've been conducting my professional and writing activities in the last year in particular has been influenced by a note of precaution.
	A financial mess is a big nuisance. A real drag. I'm hoping to brighten my reserves with the Way of the Warrior (a

projected TV series that never materialized), this book we are now embarking upon, anything else you or I can think of. I don't think I'm screwed into a position of poor man's palsy. But I don't want to do anything different from what I'm doing. I don't think I'm neurotic or inhibited or some such, or that I'm contriving <u>not</u> to make as much money as I spend.

Me   You just disagree.

{I was referring to my premise that Laing was depressed, that his current writing was too circumscribed to culminate in a best seller and that his focus on his financial problems was masking deeper problems.}

RDL   Here I am, R.D. Laing, as I stand. You <u>may</u> fulfill for me a very useful purpose. You may teach me how to become rich by just being myself. You are a very sharp, perceptive, intelligent person. You are serious. You think I'm wrong, that I'm missing something. It's very important then for me to give myself a chance to hear your input from outside of my system.

{Perhaps Laing regarded me as having business acumen; he had read my *Report* and witnessed the favorable feedback from my Self Marketing workshop participants in Italy. It was probably on the basis of this, and his awareness of my independent lifestyle, as well as my direct manner with him, that he formed this opinion.}

I continued relentlessly, directing myself to Laing's need to change his ways to insure his economic success, without satisfaction.

Me   But you don't *hear* anything.

RDL   I'm hearing it. (loudly) I've heard everything you're saying.

Me   <u>You</u> don't make sense to me. You hear me, but you don't regard what I'm saying as relevant to you. You even <u>under-stand</u> what I'm saying, in a sense, anyway, but it's not relevant to you. You think that what I'm saying is not true.

RDL   You haven't convinced me that my way of seeing myself is wrong, that my situation, and the way I put it, is wrong.

Me   I know, I know.

RDL   Or that it's not relevant.

Me   Let's do an experiment. You don't agree, you are saying, with my hypothesis that your desire for money represents a kind of pathology, a lack of participation in life by you. You work very hard, harder than anyone you know, and you are turning out what you feel is a lot of excellent material, but...

RDL   Wait a minute. You said I don't agree with your hypothesis that my desire for money represents any sort of pathology.

Me   Right. I'm paraphrasing what I think you believe. I'm not speaking for myself. I'm speaking for you.

RDL   O.K. I wouldn't use the word "desire" and I wouldn't use the word "pathology."

Me   What would you use?

RDL   I wouldn't use the connection, "represents."

Me   All right, <u>wrong</u> words. You don't believe....

RDL   It's more than wrong words. The words are the thought. I said, "I would like..." I'll accept some semantics. I would like more money coming in to Laing Enterprises. I think twice the amount would do nicely. Jutta and I would be relieved of a certain sort of problem, I think. How can I double my money without going out of my way to do so? I've given this serious thought, maybe too much, maybe I should not think about it at all for a number of months. I've put into practice a number of tactics. One is, diversity pays.

         Don't put all my eggs in one basket. So I've got all sorts of projects coming up. This is one of them. I'm open to suggestions. The pipeline in terms of publishers is not clogged. No publishers are waiting anywhere for something to publish from me.

Me   It's not that I don't try as well to lose 35 pounds. I go on diets, I do exercise. I don't think that my problem and yours are essentially different. It would be different if *I* were talking about writing a best seller. That's where *your* money comes from. That's what *you* do for a living. If you're not doing it, I think that has to do with your self-esteem. You're too arrogant to get down to addressing yourself to writing a best seller.

{At this point Ronnie called in Jutta for moral support as I had become somewhat irritating to him, and I expect that he had the thought of ending our explorations just then.}

I was elusive in this discussion, because I was afraid to suggest openly that Laing was limiting his relationship with me. Everyone in his family had free access to him while we made tapes or talked, and I felt that the level of our discussions was affected by this open door policy. I believed that there was an unspoken prohibition against alliances with anyone outside the family. My concerns, however, were a bit premature, because he did eventually include me in the spontaneity of his family's heated and intimate discussions. But on this occasion, we went another round before Laing announced that he would soon have to be going on to his next scheduled activity.

Laing, apparently not worried about short-circuiting our nascent enterprise, told me at one of our early meetings that I was irritating and intrusive. I, in turn, told him that he was defensive. I kept insisting on my point of view. He stuck to his. Could we both be right? The quest for a common metaphor was proving as elusive as the legendary quest for the Holy Grail.

We are all separated by protective shields, our defenses or egos or personalities. These shields reflect and are reflected in the organization of our thinking, our blend of the ideas and values of those who have moved us, and our reactions to these forces. Each of us has our own particular metaphor through which we filter the harsh realities of the world.

My thread of reasoning regarding Laing's objectives and defenses was delicate and tenuous because I was merely searching for some concrete behavior to attach to my pre-formed beliefs, of which I was certain. People who subscribe to theories often find themselves with this burden. I was convinced that Ronnie was somehow closed in and tightly holding on to his current family scene. His writing seemed remote, and I thought that he had very little additional energy for the creative expansion necessary for a best seller. (As it turned out, Ronnie did eventually share his obsessive concern with Jutta's betrayal, and his marriage to her would eventually culminate in divorce.) Regardless of my internal speculations, however, I was essentially saying that in spite of the exposure his fame afforded him, the content of his current writing was just not relevant enough! This idea was not congenial to him, and I knew I was on my way out.

One time, in the face of the potential opposition I represented to their belief that Laing was just not being marketed well, Jutta and Ronnie allied smoothly, picking up familiar and subtle signals from each other as they conspired to move me along to the next, less intrusive activity. They didn't seem on the road to divorce, just then. Obviously their bond went deep; they knew each other's ways. Jutta deftly suggested that I might like to meet Patricia, a resident in one of his therapeutic communities. Although Patricia turned out to be charming and fascinating, I knew that Jutta had picked up Ronnie's cue to be done with me and that she was merely carrying out his unspoken wishes.

Increasingly frustrated because my quest for a common metaphor was still unfulfilled, I was becoming less confident. It was two against one, and I knew that I did want to intrude – to be on the inside.

It was clear that my task would not be easy. Laing was neither receptive to my theoretical paradigm nor particularly interested in me. I went back to my lodgings at Huxley's flat to ponder my predicament. I wondered why Laing had invited me to come three thousand miles to discuss a project that appeared to be totally alien to him.

I was caught in a double bind: If I abandoned my objectionable confronting approach to Laing's financial quandary, I would be dishonest. If I did not, I would certainly be asked to leave. Laing did not find my opinion concerning the usefulness of his writing helpful. But if I tried to humor him or lied about my opinion, I could not test my own hypothesis: that an empathic trusting relationship between 2 well-intentioned people tends to increase one's options. In that circumstance there would not be trust. Caught between a rock and a hard place, I would have to keep on trying until my time ran out.

CHAPTER TWO

You Have To Take It Personally

The Ground Rules for Effective Confrontation

"Your friend is not a warrior," he said. "If he were, he would know that the worst thing one can do is to confront human beings bluntly."

"If one wants to stop our fellow man one must always be outside the circle that presses them, that way one can always direct the pressure."

Carlos Castenada

Feeling frustrated and perplexed at Laing's initial lack of receptiveness to my co-counseling paradigm and his lack of interest in some of the stories I had initially attempted to tell him, I consulted with Laing's old friend Francis Huxley. I was scanning my experience for some method to carry me past Laing's resistance when Francis revealingly said, "You have to take it personally." The wisdom of that seemed clear to me, and I remembered the principle of immediacy, one of my guiding ground rules for successful relationships. That is, if there's something bothering you about what the other person (your partner) is doing, find the appropriate time to confront him. Don't wait until it's no longer timely or relevant. *Timely confrontation is a way to keep a relationship fresh, honest, and real.*

Therefore, I felt called upon to tell the truth to Laing. It was not going to be easy, and it did not mean that I would abandon all tact and charm, but it did mean that if something about Laing's behavior was bothering me, I would have to find the right time and place to confront him. With considerable dread, I determined to do just that.

I must take what Laing did personally because he was my partner and possibly my friend, while at the same time I must avoid being inappropriately blunt in the encounter. The art of confrontation is a skill that is developed with practice. The challenge loomed before me. The following passage is an example of a confrontation in one of our earlier meetings, before we had arrived at a more congenial tone.

Given the nature of our project, writing a self-help book using the concept of co-counseling, making eye contact and revealing personal histories were part of the agenda. At every turn in our struggle for a common affinity I met with surprises. One surprise was an instance of Laing's total disinterest in what I was saying. Polite behavior was not his forte. This was unsettling to me and I waited to confront him....

RDL   What we may be doing is setting up a system between ourselves that is most authentic. If we play that by ear, we don't know what that system is, and it might very well not be what is formally called "co-counseling."

Me   O.K. Yesterday (*in a discussion at lunch*) you said you didn't want to be <u>entertained</u> when I was going to tell you what happened to me after I didn't eat for two weeks. (*A story I thought was quite dramatic.*) You said that what I was going to say was going to be <u>entertaining</u> and you didn't want to be entertained. Why did you say that? Why is that true?

RDL   Well, I quite often don't feel like being entertained or sitting and listening to anything <u>interesting</u> because I don't like to be interested in what someone else is saying. My interest in being interested lapses sometimes. I can become very uninterested. So I amuse myself somewhere or go for a walk.

Me   Was I doing something that particularly made you uninterested? It wouldn't be that no matter <u>who</u> was saying <u>what</u> you would be uninterested? What it made me feel like was dismissed. So maybe that's <u>my</u> problem? You're not interested in anything about me historically.

RDL   I don't expect you to be interested particularly in anything about me historically. It's a sort of inquisitiveness. I'm not interested in revealing my history particularly when I meet anyone. I meet them on the basis of their present and mine. Eventually, they might evolve a history. I might be interested in hearing all sorts of stories about you, and you might be interested in hearing all sorts of stories about me. I don't feel any therapeutic value or desire to consult with you about anything in my past. It's not particularly relevant to me in my presentation of myself to you.

Me   I think that if you were talking to someone about something, you would care if they weren't interested. I guess it just depends on who it is. It depends on your expectation. That's just how I feel.

This initial confrontation with Laing had three benefits:

1. I felt relieved having actually said something to Ronnie instead of holding in a deadening feeling of rejection and resentment.

2. I learned that Ronnie's restless attention might have more to do with him than with my intrinsic value.

3. From then on I always felt that I had his attention. Although Laing often disagreed with me, he never again stopped me from telling a story or walked away from me. Maybe this was a sign of his increased respect?

My confrontation with Laing gave me confidence. He didn't really want me to go along with him. He wanted me to express myself. This lesson would serve me well in later negotiations with him as he tended to be hard to pin down.

{Our confrontations in the initial scene at his house in Hampstead, London continued as follows. We kept disagreeing and jousting for position....}

Me   We are together and there is a goal to be accomplished—to put out something useful to people so that they can make their situations better. What I propose to you is that if we have a book we can bring up some examples.

RDL   Of what? (scratching his head and looking bemused.)

Me   Of two people who came together for something that they might otherwise have to go outside for.

Say I want to be lighter. Well, actually, since I've been here I haven't been hungry, because I'm getting something. Now you don't have to discuss what I eat. It won't make any difference because I'm getting fed someplace else. *With a more substantive food, stimulating attention, I thought.* So that's what you're saying, you just have to be natural in the right environment, and that takes care of things. You won't participate on a certain level.

RDL   I'm participating with you in the terms that I agreed to on the telephone.

Me   What are they?

Laing took out some cigaratte paper and tobacco and set them on the table in front of me. He was getting ready to roll.

RDL   As far as I can remember, they amounted to this. One way or another to get out a book, of some sort of self-help-manual order, of ways and means that would not be offensive to our tastes or other people's tastes on how people might help themselves together, as opposed to professional help. What form might we give such a book? You have your experience of co-counseling. Basically people could help each other solve their problems. And I said basically the only problem that I've got to put to you is: out of doing what I'm doing, being as I'm being, to make more money. I don't feel (laughs) that I'm on the defensive at all. Or that my history has any relevance whatever to the problem of having more to spend.

Me   You don't think so? What do you think it's due to then?

RDL   It's due to what I told you it's due to. Not enough people in the last five years have bought my books.

Me   You don't think that's anything to do with what you do? (shocked)

RDL   Well I do. (loudly) I want to continue to do what I'm doing, and I want more money. I don't want to change what I do to make more money. I want more money to come in. I told you so.

Me   Well how's that supposed to happen without your doing something?

RDL   I don't know. That's the problem <u>you</u> can address yourself to. I'm not agonizing over it. I don't see the solution to it myself.

Me   Well *I* do.

* * *

I had repeatedly told Laing that he must change his ways and do something more relevant. You may be wondering what I had in mind here, since my professed knowledge of what to do in the service of writing a best seller without Laing doing anything different seems to belie my advice to him.

Actually I had two ideas in mind:

1. I thought that if I could contextualize what was happening be-tween us skillfully enough, I could illustrate a relationship that a reader would be likely to encounter, and an illuminating self-help book could be created. Laing was, after all, being real in his relationship with me, too real for comfort. Could I really get more than that?

2. I thought that I could change him. (Don't laugh.)

I kept thinking of a subtle and profound statement by Baruch Spinoza, the seventeenth-century, Dutch-Jewish philosopher, Spinoza had said:

"If anyone conceives that he is loved by another, and he believes that he has given no cause for such love, he will love that other in return."

I was loathe to give up the idea that my love for him would change him, in spite of the fact that Laing never said he wanted to change. Notwithstanding his protestations, I never believed that he didn't want to change. Many other wistful lovers have imagined that their love would change their loved one, if only the cherished person perceived that love.

CHAPTER THREE

Consensual Validation

"To increase awareness is an absolute good."
Aldous Huxley

Formal therapeutic alliances and other healthy relationships outside of psychotherapy have a similar denouement. A point of confrontation is reached, at which time we feel each other's boundaries. This is a wonderful opportunity to let in another viewpoint and increase our awareness potential. When one is not sure whether someone else's opinion of her has any validity, one can take a poll of those who know one well.

I had used this technique both personally and in my self-marketing workshops. *Feedback can be very revealing.* After I had attributed Laing's lack of a best seller in America partly to his own lack of openness, he called Jutta in for some consensual validation.

As our conversation advanced, Laing was actively moving about the room, his library. He had elicited my feedback with regard to his financial situation. Presumably he had had more than enough of my opinion for him to digest alone.

I continued to place the responsibility for Laing's pecuniary predicament on him, and he kept up his resistant posture while inviting me to continue my onslaught.

RDL   Fine. That way you could be helpful to me.

Me   I could be. I could be, but you keep moving. It's hard. You're a moving target. (*We both laughed.*) You've got to do something different to make more money. There's a multitude of things you could do, but most of them I would not want to be part of. I think it would be "evil," as Max *(Laing's then six-year-old son)* would say, to take you away from your true calling. I think what you're supposed to be doing is looking for truth and splitting evil in two. *(Max was preoccupied with the nature of evil at that time.)* And that's what you should be getting paid for. I think *that's* what you've been paid most for when you get down to the bottom line. And a lot of other things you've been paid for, being a poet and having charm, come as a concomitant of what you did in the first place. Do you know what I mean?

RDL   Yes.

Me   I think there is a wisdom to the marketplace. You are the most famous in the world at what you do. If someone as famous as you didn't sell a book, I **wouldn't** say it was because it didn't get past the right people. It would be different if you were obscure or suddenly started writing in some strange genre. Don't forget *The Divided Self* that you wrote at twenty-eight is still in every major bookstore. What you got famous for is giving people power. You spoke out for patients that you saw were oppressed, who couldn't speak for themselves. You did that at your own personal risk. You're a doctor.

You spoke out against your profession. I think that you have in you a lot more than you've put out before, but it's on ice, on alcohol or whatever.

(I wondered how Laing would react to my reference to his drinking and braced myself in anticipation of a possible rebuke. He got up and began pacing about, fingering the books which lined the wall of the parlor.)

RDL   You're factually wrong about that. I've got a book about to come out in January (*The Voice of Experience*), and there are hundreds of books I had to read to write that. I've got a pile of manuscripts. I've got no log jam on writing.

I'm saying it's <u>there</u>. You're wrong.

Me   Well, maybe I'm wrong—-so let me read it. You're saying that your whole problem is a marketing problem. I think the thing is to turn people on as you said in *The Politics of Experience.* If you could convince people in your poetical style to do something different with somebody else, by changing their metaphors, that's very powerful. That's serving. If you could change even a small fraction of the people who read this book, then you've made an impact. When people read *The Divided Self*, they started to act differently, because they could see that something new was true. I think that's what you have to do again, and I think that is in you. But you stay away from that kind of stuff. I think there's something you could say now that would be galvanizing. I think that's what creates a best seller. It's giving readers exactly what they want. It's not just being interesting or charming. It gives them power. That's what you got famous for, giving people power. *(I concluded encouragingly.)*

RDL   Well, that wasn't in my mind when I was writing.

(So far no censure, I thought. And undaunted, I went back to the not unrelated theme of Laing's inaccessibility....)

Me   I know, you were looking for the truth. So it doesn't have to be in your mind now. But I believe that, even though some aspects of your life are fantastic—You are great with your kids, you make them strong, you play with them, you don't compete—you keep your distance all the time. And you're such a sensitive man. It's as if you are insulated. It's like a fear of getting too close. And that's what's in your way.

RDL   If it's true, I don't recognize it. I don't think that Max or Natasha or Adam *(Ronnie and Jutta's children)*, or Jutta see it that way. How could I be isolated in the sense that you say I am and have the sort of thing with Max that I have?

Me   I think sometimes you can be very close with a child, because a child is not so threatening. There are a lot of areas that don't have to be shared with them.

RDL   What are you talking about? Jutta and me, and you and me, and Leon *(Laing's psychiatrist friend, Leon Redler)* and me?

Me   Yes, I guess so. It doesn't make sense to you?

         (Silence)

RDL   Several Americans have said that to me.

Me   I don't know how to convince you.

RDL   Put it to Jutta.

Me   All right.

* * *

"I'll Have No Contract On My Eyes."

R.D. Laing

At this point Laing called Jutta into the room to test my hypothesis that he was inaccessible. Attractive, trim, unadorned, and casually dressed in a jogging outfit, Jutta was the type of woman who I imagined had never had a weight problem. She fingered her straight dark un-processed hair as she sat down next to me on the parlor couch eying the running tape recorder. Later when I asked who knew him best, Laing said he thought Jutta knew him better than anyone else did.

Asking me to put the question of his inaccessibility to Jutta, Laing continued to move about the room listening to our conversation without particularly looking at us. We proceeded....

Me	Jutta, I told Ronnie that his problem is that he has a general defense against being close to anyone. He said people say that sometimes, but they don't really understand. Psychotic people often feel very close to him, and he says they understand him. He told me to ask you the question, whether he can get close or is he inaccessible.
JL	I think he is a combination. I think one word is not enough for that. Not being close. I wouldn't put it like that. He's shy, and he's really very cautious, but I don't think he's lacking the ability to be close. I don't think he's easy to get close to... Maybe that's not right either? I mean you have to explain a little bit what you mean. Do you mean on a personal level or an intellectual level? He certainly talks about a lot of things.
Me	He talks, yes.
JL	You mean, inaccessible about a personal thing?
Me	Yes, a sort of personal inaccessibility.
	And yet, it's a contrast because his writing is the most honest of anybody I know. He's completely revealing. He puts his heart right on the page, which takes a lot of courage. And on the other hand....

JL   I think it also has to do somehow with the fact that he doesn't chat about things that make people feel closer. There's a whole chunk of verbal behavior missing which one is used to having with other people.

Me   Maybe the real question is, for yourself, do you find that Ronnie is accessible?

JL   Well, he's cautious, he's not accessible. He's not an accessible person. I don't find him accessible. (*Jutta and I laugh.*) Oh, Ronald, what are you? (*He's still wandering around silent in the room.*) Yes, I think he's cautious.

Me   So that's the answer to your question, to my question.

JL   He's a strange mixture. How would you explain what you mean by inaccessible?

Me   Well, I don't explain it well. There must be something eluding me, because I usually explain things well. But I think it's characterized most by the fact that Ronnie is always moving around. It would take him a long time to sit down and make eye contact. You know what I mean? Just hone in, that's not his style. I mean he's very close from far away. That doesn't bring out the immediacy of the situation, and at the same time he's the most honest person around. It's a paradox.

JL   But he doesn't do a few things that take the brunt off socializing like sitting next to the person who's speaking and making eye contact. Many people complain about that. You sit next to him, but his eyes totally disappear inside his head, or he will look just everywhere else except at the person who's there. And his explanation for that is that listening to someone doesn't at the same time mean that you have to look at the person. I don't know whether that's being shy, or that's a tactic, or that's a fear.

All of a sudden Laing, who had been present but silent, entered into our speculations about him, booming in, making full, intense, very close eye contact with me, causing Jutta and I to fall into paroxysms of laughter. He tried to keep us entertained, but I became a little uncomfortable with his unaccustomed proximity as Laing pushed his face almost down to mine as I sat laughing on the couch.

RDL   Have you ever looked into the Mona Lisa for twenty minutes? You feel that because someone's starting to spill out their stuff at you that you're obliged to look at them?

JL   No, no. But in ordinary conversation you do make eye contact. I agree: Even five minutes is long. But there is this thing about you with contact with people, that you have a different sort of manner, an unusual way. You're sort of a black sheep in a herd.

Although Jutta's answer supported my conclusion that Laing was inaccessible, he never explored this. Could he have remained unconvinced of his inaccessibility if his own wife thought this of him? Since he had told me that Jutta knew him better than anyone at that time, I wondered why he didn't explore this avenue of thought? I didn't ask him because he didn't seem particularly receptive to any additional feedback from me.

He remained constant no matter what I suggested. I thought he drank too much and that that was part of his inaccessibility. When I told him this without the tape recorder running, he said that he wasn't drinking any more than usual. It had never stopped him from having a best seller before. All I could do was to register my opinion periodically and press on, hoping this pressure of the "reality" I was providing would not result in a one-way ticket home.

I think Laing did think his drinking was a problem, though, because he wrote the following poem in *Sonnets*, a book which he had published in 1979:

Another one won't do me any harm.
The damage is already long since done.
I'm nothing now I've lost my funky charm.

There's no one left who knows last time I won.
There's no doubt if I alcoholize my brain
It's somehow not so bad, but still the same.
And with a little more, I can't refrain

From following my customary game.
Perhaps I'm after all not depassé.
Who knows.
I might still have it in me yet.

The best is yet to be. I know a way
To make a million dead. You want a bet?
It's time to have another round, what think?
Hey, Hello, baby! Come here! Have a drink!

Years later he discussed some of these barriers to accessibility openly and on the radio, stating that he had a problem with alcohol, but at the time of our discussion I had to content myself with moving on to setting up a system that would work for us.

At this juncture Laing ended the session saying that he had to go on to his next appointment. Laing and I passed each other making unusually close eye contact as I went through his front door. I was clearly on my way out. There were plenty of polite salutations now, more than I wanted.

"Do you still want to do it?" I said haltingly from a distance of about ten inches.

Laing said that he wanted to go on with another meeting, but his obligation to try to work with me would then be fulfilled. He would call the next morning to confirm our final hour.

"I have one caveat though," I said cannily. "Could we have our meeting at Huxley's house, with the door closed and no interruptions?" He agreed, but it was to be only for an hour—he had a full day of work, seeing clients, writing, and a board meeting concerning his therapeutic community, he said.

We were not off to a promising start. Laing seemed mercenary and querulous. I was self-absorbed and combative. The gold of empathy was still a buried treasure.

CHAPTER FOUR

Joining the Resistance

"Tend to the patients according to their wants and their needs."
Anonymous

After our heated exchange, I thought my time with Laing might be very limited. Instead of the constructive partner I had hoped to be, in the service of integrity, I was fast becoming quite the opposite—both an irritant and an accuser. *Attack only produces counterattack* and distancing. I didn't want either and was in a double bind. If I stopped telling what I thought was the truth, how could I be real in our relationship? If I stopped being honest, how could I be constructive? If I continued in that vein, how could I avoid jeopardizing our relationship?

Because I imagined that the end for our embryonic project was at hand, I stayed up all night trying to solve this problem. Ensconced in an environment conducive to high and hard thinking, among Francis and Julian Huxley's books, I sat before the fire pondering the progress of this project and my fate.

Well into the night an idea suddenly came to me and I was infused with a feeling of great relief. ***Join the resistance:*** That was the answer. If Laing felt that marketing was what he needed, why not help him with it? Maybe this was the area of concern he was most comfortable in addressing? Maybe I was just being insensitive? Did it really matter that this was not the project I came for? I would have hated to go home to New York City having had a negative effect and the feeling that I was right, but without any project—a Pyrrhic victory indeed.

Ronnie confirmed our appointment the next day for one hour in the morning. If we could not work out a viable plan, this was to be our last meeting. It would take place at Huxley's house in a private setting, instead of in Laing's study where we were subject to the unplanned interruptions of his family's day-to-day activities. Set and setting always convey a message.

With the door closed, we sat down before the fire at Huxley's house, and the following crucial dialogue transpired:

Me   You're right. I figured out that what I should do is treat your pleasure in earning twice the money as if it were my pleasure in weighing 35 pounds less. Let's switch! I'll make it an area of central concern to myself and use whatever I know in the service of achieving that goal. I'll make a game plan whether my initial concept (of co-counseling to increase our options) is correct or not. And it doesn't really matter, because even if it's correct, this will only help anyway. What do you think?

I didn't view this approach as lacking integrity. It was intended to be an adjustment to enable me to work with Laing at a level which was congenial to him. I did not feel compromised, even though this was not my view of our original agreement. On the contrary, I was happy to serve him.

RDL   All right, go ahead.

Me   So, to make a game plan, if I were doing business, I would say, let's make a list of all the possible products or services you want to market, and then we'll create a marketing plan.

We will have goals with time limits. After one month, we should have received a certain amount of income based on projections. Let's say we'll have a monthly checkpoint, and have all the different projects listed under what actual behaviors or marketing strategies are appropriate for each project. We're going to review them in a month. If we haven't met our projected goals, we'll correct our course. And if it's still on, we'll just move forward, as you would with any marketing plan. I'll familiarize myself as much as possible with everything that you think is worth selling, and furthermore, if I can come up with anything that's unique, a different slant, based on your natural capacities, I will suggest it.

RDL   Well, I've got a very good agent, or at least I think he is. He markets what I produce to publishers, whatever I'm produc-ing. I've got a bank manager. He expects to get from me that sort of projected run-down on income in the next three to six months. So I don't see what you mean, "if you'll look at this, we'll correct our course."

Me   What I mean by that is, we're going under the assumption that you don't want to do anything different. You're putting out what you're putting out. If it's sold properly to American audiences, your income would double in a certain time frame. That's the goal. Right?

I was joining him and restating his position.

RDL   Yes.

Me   That's the goal. We have to ask ourselves, "What is being sold?, to whom? And how can we increase their receptive-ness to it? How can it best be exposed to the right audience?" It could be in the way of packaging; that's what marketing is about, target presentation.

RDL   Obviously, I don't want to know anything about that, since that's not my function, as exemplified by the format of marketing.

Me   Yes.

RDL   As an author I'm not expected to and shouldn't sit in on these meetings.

Me   Yes. Then how would you suggest that I might serve?

RDL   Well, I still think the thought behind your coming over here is a very good idea, which is to produce a book that will make a lot of money.

Me   But, you don't want to use us as an example of people in the book, as I originally suggested. Is that what you're saying? I'm not negating that. I'm for it, and that's what I thought would be produced as far as us being together. But that's a style that's irksome to you. And you're telling me that you want me to come up with ideas. So I figure that if I serve you and you serve me, that's an example of what we're telling other people to do from the message of our book. We're telling the reader to find somebody who's got the wherewithal, to develop a system with her, and take on the other person's problems, and potentially that would be curative or get you what you want. It would help to break you out of the preoccupation with your own problems. So we'll be documenting it and also making a book out of it. We are in the book as well.

RDL   It won't break this aspect of the problem unless the book makes money.

Me   Yes.

RDL   How do we make best use of the time we spend together?

Me   I think the best way to make money out of the time spent together is to produce a book that encourages people to spend time with somebody else, and focus on the other person instead of themselves, thereby releasing themselves from the trap of being demoralized and just honed in on their own problems. I thought we'd set an example doing the same thing. I don't have to become an author, but you don't want especially to have these meetings as a procedure for revealing yourself or doing the things I originally suggested. I want to see the reason in that. We could just talk about whatever...what you would need from me. I could say what I need from you.

RDL   That in itself is not going to make a book that other people will buy, because this problem may be irrelevant to other people. Showing how I can make money out of writing is not going to help Tom, Dick, and Harry make money. That's not everyone's problem, and that's not the main problem most people are involved with. Obviously it's going to be used as a pretext for a morality tale. In this respect, in terms of these conversations, you paid far more attention to me so far, trying to beat any problem I've got, than I have in terms of what you've told me.

Me   I'll tell you anytime you want. (hopefully)

RDL   I don't think protestations about hearing it will put me very much in the mood. Try it out and see.

I couldn't believe that he finally would listen to me. He knew almost nothing about my personal history and hadn't shown the slightest bit of curiosity about my past experiences. The potential benefits to be derived from his active attention seemed like a pool in the desert to me. Since my heretofore most insightful friend, Richard, had died the year before, I was desperate to connect. My story was unconventional and easy to misunderstand and I therefore considered sensitive understanding to be a most treasured gift. I felt that Laing would be consistently able to judge my intent and not be misled by appearances.

At Ronnie's long-awaited and almost reluctant invitation, I launched into a concentrated version of my life story — racing the clock to avoid sparing any meaningful details in what I thought might be the last time I saw him. I never stopped for air, but my eyes were on him as he stretched out before the fireplace, seeming to disappear into what I was saying. He closed his eyes. I felt that he was listening with a power of floating, unfettered attention that I had never before had the privilege to be awarded. I felt free to say anything and had the sensation of a veil lifting. There was no censor here. How had he established that? Was it just my projection?

This is a sacred space, I thought. And on I went, directing a rush of words to this tired man, stretched out before the fireplace, listening with what seemed to be all of his attention.

Me   Yes. Somehow I <u>feel</u> more here, because I'm just not hungry. You know, when I was a child, I used to sit with my father. He was very sensitive and didn't say a lot.... He was kind of accepting. Unlike you, he didn't communicate with a lot of people, but he communicated with me. He used to sit in his Barcalounger and read books all the time. He was not formally educated, but he'd read Bertrand Russell and other philosophers, and he'd share ideas with me. Sometimes he'd come upstairs to the attic where I lived, and I thought it thrilling for him to come up to me. He'd tack a quote, full of meaning, on my bulletin board and not even talk about it. (*The Bertrand Russell quote about intimacy at the beginning of chapter one was among them.*) Then the quote would be central to me. So it was extremely exciting to be around him. We always shared ideas. None of the boys at school were as exciting.

In a way, I felt I had an exclusive relationship with my father in that we understood each other so well. But, of course, he wasn't going to marry *me*.

My mother's sensibilities were of a different order. As sensitive as my father was, she was the opposite. Whenever we had a discussion around the dinner table, there were several levels of conversation. Implications meant more than outright statements.

I'd come home every day and tell him what happened, and when I was very fond of a boy my age he was always critical. He had an investment in my staying with him, since he wasn't really communicating with anyone else as well.

When I was twenty, I decided I was going to leave home because I would be done in by staying there. Nevertheless, I felt that I was very central in that house. My father, mother, and brother each needed me in their own ways. I went off to graduate school in Norman, Oklahoma to study clinical psychology. I felt guilty for leaving. I thought they would somehow self-destruct.

Anyway, my father became ill with cancer soon after I left. He couldn't say anything but my name. He was dying. The doctors said he had about two weeks to live.

When I had gone off to graduate school my father hadn't helped me with expenses because he didn't want me to go away. I knew he was going to die when I left even though he was not ill at the time. I just looked at him as I left him at the airport, and I was sure the whole family was going to fall apart, but I thought I would die if I stayed. When he got sick I came back to New York and stayed with him. All of my immediate family did die over the course of a few years. For a long time I didn't pursue ideas because I was angry with my father, because I had left school and come back when he got sick to sit at his hospital bed. He wanted me to stay with him, just me—not my mother. He didn't want her to visit him in the hospital even after all their years together. She wasn't allowed to come and see him.

I became the head of the household, in a way. My thirteen-year-old brother was disturbed by all this. He wanted to leave home and join us (*my father and me*). So when I was twenty, I was in a metaphorical sense "married" to my father, had a child (my brother), and virtually killed my mother by uniting with my ailing father and brother to deprive her of her role of wife and mother. I knew she wouldn't love me anymore, but I felt I owed it to my father to be with him because he had stayed in his tempestuous marriage for my sake.

He went back to her after a while, leaving me to deal with the repercussions. She promptly put my father in a home where he died several years later. I was angry with him because I felt betrayed. I stopped reading anything serious (that had to do with the ideas we had discussed) for about ten years. When my mother died a few years later, I felt very sad and stayed in bed for a long time.

By that time I was married. My husband was used to my being strong and self-reliant, and he was impatient with my lying there, although I was still marginally taking care of my business. My brother, unable to cope with life, died a few years after that.

Finally I got up one day and decided that this was <u>not</u> what I was going to do. I did not want to die. So I picked up where I left off with my father. I started arranging my life to be as free as possible to study. That ultimately brought me here for some reason. (*slight pause*)

Laing hadn't moved, nor had he interrupted. His eyes were still closed. I felt that he was conspiring with me, not sleeping, and on I went.

In the course of events, though, in order to get divorced, I went into therapy for four years and I got slim. (I had become overweight while married.) When I got slim, the world became very erotic. I didn't have enough experience.

I had been married for over seven years, and faithful. Life became traumatic. I didn't really know how to handle things.

It was frightening to me. I picked men who were no more available to me than my father had been. They used me because I was capable and lent myself to that. They were exciting. But I guess I got scared and then got somewhat heavier again. I didn't like myself. I was stuck and depressed, and I spent my time wandering about the house, attached to the telephone like an umbilical cord, with an enormous support system that didn't really mean anything except as an emotional fix. I still eat too much—-another fix. I'm thirty-five pounds too heavy.

Me   The thought of being able to serve you in some way gives me a purpose again, the same purpose that I stopped having with my father. So as soon as you picked up on this project for real in July, I got very elated. I began to feel fulfilled. I have piles of notebooks from my studies about what makes people feel loved, what makes them feel happy, what makes other people love them. I guess it's what I'm looking for in a certain sense. I don't know where that goes. You make me feel good, because you are so sensitive and because you have courage.

I began studying therapy and motivation, I befriended different professors. Using my headhunting skills, I made them interested in teaching me. Mostly, because I would just give them what they wanted and be their friend. It was as if I had gone back to ten years before, when I was still chasing ideas with my father. I thought I could find and attach myself to anybody I wanted. I felt powerful. I was looking to discover the principles of behavior, and I started to make a list of them. I wanted to replace my family. Of course, I had free time and economic freedom, because my business of executive recruiting was lucrative, and studying was an adventure. So I wound up collecting all sorts of captivating people from different walks of life and induced them to love me in whatever way they were capable and in whatever way I needed. And I learned from them.

So...I compiled a list of principles that work to earn friendship. Somewhere inside I feel that if I love someone, there's no one I can't reach, because I won't take rejection as rejection. I'll take it as resistance, I just used whatever metaphor moved me forward toward the goal of proximity. Now I have started to reach a wider range of people. I've been interviewed on TV and by some reporters. Life is more intense and exciting.

But still it lacks that....It doesn't lack it—if I serve you. It doesn't lack it—but everything will work out fine.

What I learned by looking into this therapy setup is that if you get somebody who gives a damn and create some sort of system—it doesn't really matter which system it is, psychoanalysis, writing a book together, or any game you want to play—but a system that kind of locks you in with a commitment, and when the person is compatible with you conceptually and with your values, you can make enormous strides. I think most people suffer from a kind of demoralization that manifests itself in lack of money, or keeping oneself unattractive or lonely, all forms of crippling behavior.

I think it's the trip that you take with someone else that empowers you to act. I would love to be together with somebody, but I don't want to be untrue. I'd like to have a baby. I'm thirty-seven, so I have to do that, if I'm going to, within a couple of years, I think. What do you think?

RDL   Oh, (sigh) it depends on what terms I suppose you set for yourself. You want to be with someone and be free and have a baby.

Me   And skinny, too!

RDL   Yes. (Both laugh)

Me   And I adore you. I think you are so fabulous.

At this point Ronnie asked me to join him, just then, at a meeting of the board of the Philadelphia Association, an organization that directed the home he ran for those recuperating from the hardships of life and from depersonalizing mental health institutions. He also asked me to attend a party for the house later that evening and invited me to begin the work of our book in earnest with him the next day.

As we closed our fateful, but brief, meeting together, he told me that cure in Latin is "curo," which originally meant to take care of or attend to. Obviously, I was now in good hands, and I knew it. I experienced an unusual lightness and my heart was singing.

This was a lot to reveal to him in one sitting. No one had ever listened to me limitlessly, in an unstructured setting — not even a therapist, but he had risen to my need.

Once he understood me, I felt he was caught by his heart. I knew he would never leave me. The severed link was tied. I now felt connected as I had when my father had been alive and had wanted me to fulfill our mission.

Our mission had been in the form of an amorphous quest to learn— about which I had written long before in the following poem:

Imprint

Blissed out on Miltowns and
Bertrand Russell's ideas
my father read books in his big green Barca Lounger
with Gaslight Review playing soft music on his
        Grundig radio.
We'd stay up late and talk.

Even when he couldn't read anymore
he held his book upside down before him
waiting for the answers
he sent me out to find.

In the early days when we were first setting the tone for our relationship, Jutta, Ronnie, and I sat around their long wooden kitchen table having tea. The table looked out through tall glass doors onto their backyard garden. Attempting to make me feel at home, Laing, pointing to the refrigerator and cupboards with a generous sweeping gesture, told me to help myself to food anytime I wanted. I felt harbored like a patient in Gheel.[1] Jutta, looking annoyed, quickly reestablished control of her domain, the kitchen, by a restraining remark. Laing and I both jerked to the bit immediately, exchanging knowing smiles with each other.

During the next six weeks, instead of expelling me as I had feared, Ronnie became increasingly receptive, tuned in to me, and candid about himself. As he became more comfortable with me, he also became more illogical and thereby reached the creative frame of mind in which he did best. Thus he fulfilled the prediction he had made on our initial meeting at Huxley's house.

A Serendipitous Coincidence

My stay in Huxley's Hampstead home turned out to be the basis of a serendipitous event.

During my sixteenth summer I was fascinated with issues of free will and scientific determinism, without knowing the formal names of these opposing belief systems. I had read a little-known book by Mark Twain entitled *What is Man?* In it, Twain says that man is a machine, everything is caused by a prior cause and there is only the illusion of free will. I was struck with this idea because it shook the foundations of my thinking. I wondered how there could be an all-knowing God who

---

[1] Gheel was a town renowned for its unique system of family care for the mentally ill. When a fourteenth century sickroom in a town in Northern Belgium became too crowded the patients were lodged in the home of the inhabitants. In 1850, this religious-municipal system became a medically supervised establishment. Traditionally, patients in Gheel have been taken into protective custody.

punished and rewarded people for doing merely what he had programmed them to do. It seemed to be an extraneous and silly idea.

I asked my father, who simply sent me out to find the answer, presumably at Queens College where I was to be a freshman that fall. After consulting with priests, pastors and rabbis (to my parent's chagrin) and without finding satisfactory answers, I eagerly arranged for an appointment with the acting head of the department of philosophy at Queens College. I asked her for the names of authors who refuted the idea that man was a machine, and told this academic authority—my first contact with a college professor—that the systems whose validity I had previously accepted, such as capital punishment, made no sense if the assumption that everything is caused and therefore there is no free will were true. The acting department head agreed with my radical philosophical deductions, but asked not to be quoted. In the service of my quest she recommended the author, Julian Huxley. I searched the Queens College library in vain, finding only biology books by Julian Huxley, but no answers to my questions about the existence of free will or about God's possible reasons for praising or punishing his own creations. After my sixteenth year had passed, my "burning" questions took a back seat to more practical matters.

You may imagine my sense of awe when 21 years later I found myself sequestered in Francis Huxley's house where Laing had arranged for me to stay while working with him in London. Francis was the son of the late Julian Huxley. Sir Julian Huxley's books were on his shelves, and there, and while looking through them, I discovered quite serendipitously, the answer to my long-buried question about the existence of God and His mystifying behavior. In the book *Religion Without Revelation* Huxley wrote, "Raw materials out of which religions are formed consist of actual religious experiences, numinous or holy, metaphysical or transcendent." He said that the term divine did not originally imply the existence of gods; on the contrary, he said, gods were constructed to interpret man's experiences of this quality. The divine is what compels man's awe.

I *was* awed. Where had Julian Huxley found the strength and perspective to rise above the accepted religious systems of his times with such clarity? How could I have been so lucky to have made this discovery and have Laing to share it with as well? Back in New York City in the business world I hadn't found a big demand for this type of inquiry.

The next day when I told Laing of my numinous experience, he understood completely, and that evening we went out to a neighborhood pub, and he celebrated with me. He was very ready to share his personal history there. He told me, among other things, that his father had been intrigued with Julian Huxley, too.

I was delighted to have found the intellectual playmate I had had in my father, and I felt like Robinson Crusoe discovering footprints in the sand. A seed that had been planted but had been dormant until now was just waiting to bear fruit. Laing also had the advantage of a broad-based classical education. He was an original thinker, who moved easily in the world of ideas. He said he was allergic to transference, though. That should have been a warning, but I didn't see him breaking out in any rashes, and he seemed to be welcoming more and more of my companionship. He was becoming a confidant.

After two weeks of daily meetings with Laing, I returned home to New York City to process what we had discussed and to write. Two weeks later I was back in London working daily with him on our book. By the end of a month together, Ronnie was frequently inviting me to share in the warmth, spontaneity, and turbulence of his family, and in the last week, we spent thirty hours together, just living, working on the book, sharing stories, and hanging out with his friends and family. By this time Laing had told me the painful details of his situation with Jutta. He said that I might already be aware that Jutta had a lover. I said I was aware of it. He said that he was planning to leave Jutta and sell the house, but not just yet. The clandestine had become commonplace, but it seemed to me that his pain had not lessened. When Jutta and Laing went out, Laing often invited me along. Why I fit in so easily with them was now more apparent: My unabashed adoration of Laing must have been a salve to his wounds.

One evening, Ronnie invited me to join him and Jutta at the New Vic Theater where they were performing together; he, among other poets, was to read a selection of his poetry and then play a piano accompaniment for Jutta who was to sing at this engagement.

While I was waiting by myself in the crowded lobby for the formalities of the evening to begin, a young man who had been supervised by R.D. Laing during his psychotherapy training engaged me in a conversation. When we eventually introduced ourselves, I was amazed to find out that he already knew of me and furthermore had even read my book. This was astonishing because the book, my *Report on Effective Psychotherapy*, had been published by my own company and marketed by both me and Atcom, a New York publisher of professional newsletters. Although some university libraries and psychology professionals had bought it in America, I hardly imagined that it had reached the English market. I was surprised and happy that it had somehow been conveyed to this psychiatrist-in-training and asked him how it had come to his attention. He told me that when he had asked Laing what psychotherapy was really all about, Laing had handed him the *Report* and told him to read it. This psychiatry student felt that it had clarified psychotherapy for him. Laing had never mentioned recommending my book to a student. I was both thrilled and astonished. Although becoming more confident, I was still on the lookout for signs of Laing's regard.

Later on, when I asked Laing what he thought of me, he told me that he thought I was smarter than I thought I was. I had a field day with that one! Occasionally he would praise me to Jutta. Jutta began to enter the room more frequently when we were recording our customary conversations, often dusting the furniture or fluffing pillows. Laing, smiling, would say, "Oh, Jutta."

By this time, I thought Laing was my best audience. (Incidentally, this is what my mother had always said about my father.) I thought my mother would not have been entirely displeased if I had been married and out of the house by 16. However, I didn't want to push my luck in London; Laing's uncommon attention to me was inviting notice.

Laing's confidences came more frequently. He would sometimes ask my opinion about Jutta's behavior and his reaction to her. Once, using psychological jargon, I responded: "With the narcissistic personality, joining is the method of choice." This titillated him for hours. He enjoyed having a devoted pal around the house.

Ultimately when my love for Laing was becoming overwhelming, it was Jutta I told first, not Ronnie. Jutta, a safe recipient of this disclosure, smiled smugly and told me that although many women had fallen in love with Ronnie, no one else had ever come to her with the news. She therefore seemed to trust me, and we shared our own good times, as well as going around with Ronnie together. Actually Jutta felt for the most part that I was good for Ronnie; she thought that our self-help book would be successful and read the installments as they emerged. Even though Laing was not at the center of Jutta's romantic interests (interests which she did discuss with me), she did not want him to lose interest in her.

I was not unacquainted, however, with what Freud had labeled **repetition compulsion,** *which dooms the driven character to act out the same disastrous behavior over and over again. I wanted to be sure that there wasn't even a hint of betrayal here. Years before I had incurred my mother's wrath by helping my ailing father to stay away from her. From the time of my divorce in 1975, I had been most driven by men who were in some very significant way otherwise engaged. At this milestone I did not want to be branded as the other woman and ousted, particularly since my love affair at that space in time consisted entirely of talk and wishful thinking.*

During this whole period I felt intensely alive and fully engaged. I felt as if I were being eaten and my ideas either spit out or digested. Laing was brilliant and quixotic, but not easy. By then, it seemed to me that a quality of purity suffused everything Laing did.

Every so often I had the benefit of Francis Huxley's consultation. I felt enriched by his erudition, charmed by his British accent replete with trilled r's and buoyed up by the shared experience of his long and difficult friendship with Laing. When Laing got too testy, I found Francis' feedback comforting. There in Hampstead, London, I felt euphoric.

Laing seemed free of duplicity. It was as if he talked to me in my own voice. I knew I was not evil — though I had been led to consider this possibility because my entire family had self-destructed in the wake of my departure from them. And all along I had had the benefit of a strong sense of mission. I thought of myself as a warrior. What better thing could I be doing than helping to bring R.D. Laing out to more people in the world? Of course, I hoped the benefits would turn out to be mutual.

* * *

CHAPTER FIVE

Setting Up A System

"If you face life consciously and use all your mental resources, knowledge, reason and imagination, sensitivity, capacities for wonder and love, for comprehension and compassion, for spiritual aspiration and moral effort, you may very well succeed."

Julian Huxley

Me   Do you want to set up a structure?

RDL   Of our interchange?

Me   Yes, encompassing and sharing much of what we have learned about living. I was thinking, it's really teaching people how to have a symbiotic relationship. It's different from therapy in the sense that it's actually more customized and selective. Therapists often select patients by their ability to pay and to abide by the rules. In our system, the reader might select someone who elicits natural feelings of affection or admiration in them. We would tell people that one way to handle the difficulties they may have is to ***invest in someone else and work out a system around a project that is useful to both of you, and work out some constructive ground rules.***

RDL   Tell me, what is the difference between this and what has already been written about co-counseling?

Me   You're saying, what's the difference between co-counseling in the generic sense and this proposition?

RDL   Yes.

Me   Symbiosis, for one thing; when you quit, it doesn't have to be part of the cure as in therapy or co-counseling. Here you might just wind up friends.

        We pick someone who has some relevant contribution to make in an area we particularly want to engage in. That makes it more specific an arrangement than if we were just looking for accord.

        If you are going to do something out of the ordinary, you would need a special set of expectations for yourself....You don't want to fall back on some former behavior that hasn't worked so well before. When you select a person you think might be helpful to you, you will then make some arrangement with that person. We are assuming that this will contradict behavior patterns that ordinarily prevent you from making closer contact or keeping a contract like this.

        To give you a specific example: When I first became interested in acquiring more friends, because I had gone through so many changes in my intimate relationships in a relatively short time, I felt that I probably didn't know how to earn these selected friendships without a special effort. This may be irrelevant to some people, but I needed something that would change me, so that I would have more staying power. So I made up a story for myself, and the story was that I was a therapist; then whatever the other chosen person did which was negative to me, I would see it as resistance. I didn't say I was a therapist explicitly.

That metaphor, thinking of myself as a therapist, had a lot of error in it, because it's skewed for an acquisitive style which is not always desirable. But it corrects the tendency to run away from other people and increases the likelihood of attracting them. It helped to combat some of my self-defeating metaphors at a time when I was particularly vulnerable. (The twenty-two steps that I used as a guide for my "therapist stance" are noted here in the chapter entitled "The Acquisition Mode.")

If you set up a metaphor for yourself, it should be whatever you're comfortable with; it doesn't have to be of the therapist mode. You may need to run away <u>more</u> or to pay <u>more</u> attention to your symptoms. Just filter your experience in some way that will allow you to do something different, to try out some behavior more in line with your goals. In other words, part of this is taking responsibility. You are effectively a teacher. You just do this to get yourself going. People have difficulty in that area in the first place. It's like stalking your own behavior. You look for the errors in your thinking and try to correct for them.

RDL   Stalking?

Me   Stalking your own behavior, watching it. You take apart the mistakes that prevent you from getting what you want. I see our plan as different from regular co-counseling in its specificity and its creativity. You can make it operational once you get the relationship going. If you assume that you will get more power, you will go out and do your thing.

Co-counseling mostly, I think, just gets the relationship going, but it doesn't have specific results-oriented tasks in the real world. It's sort of like half a partnership. *Before setting up a system with someone it might be beneficial*

to get a clear-eyed look at your own story so that you may
see how you might like to redirect the plot.

The House System

That evening, after a six hour day of therapy, and a book-recording session with me, Laing gave me a sample of his brand of therapy in action. He took me to a party at 95 Mayfield Rd., one of the London households that was a successor to Kingsley Hall, the original therapeutic community that he founded in the 60s. As the unpaid Chairman of the Philadelphia Association, Laing would meet weekly in one of these houses and *be* with its occupants.

That night he played delightful and haunting music on the piano there. He took requests and Cole Porter show tunes were his specialty of the house. They, the people living in the house who had found life on the outside a living hell, those people, sang, they danced, they talked, they ate, they smoked, they drank wine. The people who lived in the house loved Laing and he loved them. They were not stigmatized or treated or talked down to or categorized. They just were. He had told me that he was more at home with them than with others at most other social gatherings.

Laing's friends Leon Redler and Francis Huxley were there too, sitting in a circle, cross-legged on the floor, with the others, telling stories. They had done this many times before and seemed to be enjoying themselves.... Several people sat at a large table in the kitchen and ate savory stew which an in-house resident had made for them. The place smelled like a home, not a hospital. Laing was deeply engrossed in conversation with a messed-up-looking young man who was a resident there.

I walked over, listened for a while, and made a comment to Laing. I don't remember what I said to him, but I know he heard me. He never even picked his head up to look at me and answer. I noticed a faint hint of a smile appear on the young man's face. This was his time. He was important. Ah, yes. That was therapy. I never loved Laing more than I did at that moment. He cared.

Unfortunately, it was not until 1992, while reading a book called *Community Mental Health Principles and Practices*, co-authored by Ronnie's friend Dr. Loren Mosher and his associate Dr. Lorenzo Burti that I began to learn some of the complex reasons that therapeutic places like this did not attract greater numbers. I had thought I knew more than I did know.

CHAPTER SIX

Pull Out Your Poison Arrow

"Man is condemned to be free; because once thrown into the world he is responsible for everything he does."

Jean-Paul Sartre

As we grow up and pursue our own interests, people around us are hurt by our departures and reallocations of energy and affections. So, inadvertently, sometimes with the best of intentions, we still hurt those we love in the process of our own development. Being human, we feel guilty. There are a few exceptions: psychopaths and saints. Martin Buber wrote that hurting others and subsequently feeling guilty is the human condition.

When feeling guilty, we may try to serve some other person to make up for the damage we have caused, particularly if the original victim of our privation is not available for compensation. Laing seemed to be the perfect person for me to serve and thereby make amends for some of the pain I had inadvertently caused my family by leaving them when they still needed me. The Christian tradition views this phenomenon through the lens of original sin, with subsequent expiation to bring us closer to fulfilling our potential. One may expiate one's "sins" by serving. For example, if you feel guilty about being less loving than you would have liked to be toward your mother, you might find a friend in your current reality who could benefit from your ministrations. In a more extreme instance: If a child had died through your actions, taking in a homeless child might provide redemptive and regenerative feelings and effects.

In the looking-glass of psychoanalytic theory people are said to act out and repeat compulsions. We may become trapped in the same guilt provoking drama until we have worked through the compulsive behavior and made this unconscious process conscious. At this juncture we often find the cure. We may no longer need to pick punishing mates or stay in jobs that don't challenge us or carry on a life inundated with compulsive eating or drinking. Ideally, we "do over" the guilt-provoking act symbolically by acting it out as a drama, dissipating the guilt, and making our unconscious behavior more conscious as we go. Ultimately, we have the "cure" which heralds a new phase of freer and more expansive activity.

I was stalking my behavior vigilantly, always on the watch for recurrent patterns lurking in Laing's and my unfolding saga. Therefore, I did write out my own story to keep track of any occurrence of the hoped-for variations on my own theme of expulsion and isolation. I wanted to alter self-defeating behavior by finding requited love and losing the extra pounds I was carrying.

My father had gone back to my mother after I had alienated her and her family in the service of complying with my father's request to stay with him in what I thought were his final days. My father had finally left me to bear the scorn of an outcast while he returned to my mother. I, in turn, dreaded the possibility of being used by Laing merely to get a rise out of Jutta and then being abandoned. This unlikely occurrence would have broken my heart. I trusted Laing. He knew what I was afraid of, and he had a good heart. I was ready for a happy ending.

{This conversation took place in 1981 after R.D. Laing told me that my results were a poor example of the success of my method, since I still needed to lose the thirty-five pounds. I explained that I had been successful before with my suggested method, but it and I still needed more work.}

Me   You know I have been a lot fatter. Not all my life, but when I was married I got very fat to the point where I couldn't buy clothes in a regular store. This had never happened to me before. All through college I looked fine, and I didn't know what to do later when I suddenly got very heavy. I was panicked. I felt like a freak. And I figured it was hopeless; I just really didn't know what to do, and so I had to make a decision. And I went back and forth....I have faith, I guess, and a sense of timing, I suppose. I didn't think that it would take too much longer to get over that phase. I knew what I needed. I have notebooks dating back to seven years ago which say what I'm looking for, written like a game plan. I wanted someone who could **talk** to me. I couldn't find anyone to really communicate with in the way that I wanted to. It wasn't that people weren't talking to me. It was a qualitative thing. And it's very important to me, I guess. That's the most important thing.

      I also wanted to communicate better in writing. What could I do about that? For a long time there was no interoffice communication, since I worked by myself. There was almost nobody I wrote to in a formal way, and I hadn't practiced much in the way of written communication since graduate school in 1966. I figured there were areas of inadequacy I'd have to make up for by doing things that were difficult. But if that's what I wanted, I would just break it down into steps. Even if I was at a point that didn't warrant too much celebration, I could at least feel that I was on a path to something more. Most people make up stories to themselves, don't you think? To keep themselves on a target?

RDL   Um...I don't know. Yes, I think that must be true. Once somebody gets into starting to tell you about themselves in whatever way that is, it's a story. It's difficult to tell what a story is in a way, but it's—without getting too fancy about that—in a simple-minded way, it's a story. Some people seem to have so much debris in their life that they can't even spin a passion out of the debris as they tell it. I mean, they're an extreme case in point, you might say. People tell us stories in railway compartments and on airplanes and in pubs and so on. Someone will launch into a number; it's their story. It's difficult to tell how many people you might say are aware of their story.

Me   So maybe we could have them **put it down.**

RDL   For themselves. I mean, **look at it.**

Me   Yes. **Make a little assessment.**

RDL   I think that's a good task for some people. It serves them right. (Laing smiling sardonically.)

Me   It couldn't hurt. (smiling back and feeling joined.)

RDL   **Put your story down and have a good look at it.** I don't know how many people look at their own stories. I've had thousands of stories sent to me through the mail. I've got several box files of letters from people who, having read *The Divided Self*, *The Facts of Life*, or *The Politics of Experience*, or other books of mine, or after I had appeared to them in a dream, have launched into twenty pages or more of <u>their</u> story. If the right person came along to make a selection of them (I'm not for that myself at present), there's a great book there.

There's two classes of people. There are the people that your advice is meant for, who are what you would call extroverts. They can do it without getting it into their heads that they're disobeying the laws of God or the Protestant ethic or the work ethic or the Messianic code by withdrawing from the immediate field of battle and retiring themselves from the front line, if possible, for a bit, to collect themselves, take stock of the situation, and use their gumption.

Whether they're in business, in offices, in the uniformed services, wherever they could use their God-given intelligence whoever they are, in whatever mode they've developed it, and apply it, in the service of God.

Me   That's it. Use their best system to work for them.

RDL   There's two classes of people. There are the people that your advice is meant for, who are what you would call extroverts. They can do it without getting it into their heads that they're disobeying the laws of God or the Protestant ethic or the work ethic or the Messianic code by withdrawing from the immediate field of battle and retiring themselves from the front line, if possible, for a bit, to collect themselves, Use "it," which God has given them, to use on their own problems. *Lay out the problem.* It's very difficult to see a problem when it's behind your eyes. Lay it out. *Type it out or write it out. Look at it*, if possible, dispassionately. You can look at it with such narcissistic bonding as to bring tears to your eyes, or grimaces of distaste at what you see. After each paroxysm of self-pity or self-disgust or self-adulation, look at it again and again, and again until those tears are dry, the laughter has subsided, the sobs have ceased. Then look at it, quite dispassionately, as though it were a piece of writing by someone else, coming from the other side of the page completely.

Me   That's a very interesting thing to do.

RDL   Until you've got nothing to do with it at all. Look at it from the outside. Yes, it's a salutary exercise. Do it as if you've been outside of your skin in the first place.

Me   We should try this exercise. {No response from Laing, but on he went.}

RDL   Look at your own bleeding heart, from the outside, on the paper.

Me   Be your own consultant.

RDL   Yes. And give yourself the best advice you could if you were operating a Dear Abby column. First of all, take it. If you don't take it, ask yourself why you're not taking it.

Me   Right.

RDL   But first of all, take it. Having taken it, do not <u>assume</u> you have taken it, and do not talk yourself out of it. Some people go on asking themselves why they're not taking their own advice. One of the "reasons" they're not taking their own advice, is that they're asking themselves why they're not.

Me   And they're not answering.

RDL   If they'd just stop <u>asking</u> themselves.

Me   And take it. Yes!

RDL   There's a reverberating Buddhist story. The Buddha is talking about removing pain. Many people are like the chap who has a poison arrow stuck in him. He comes to you and asks you for your advice and you tell him, "You've got a poison arrow in you, pluck it out." He says, "Well, yes, but before I pluck it out, I would like to know who shot it, and whose fault it is that it's sticking in me and anyway, I don't believe that it's poison—You prove to me that it is. I would like a lab test to determine it." By the time he's got all his questions asked, let alone answered, he's dead.

          "Just take it out," the Buddha said. "Then we can examine the wound, clean it. You'll recover. Then we can look into how it got there. Was it your fault or the archer's fault or no one's fault? Was it Karma, whether it was this or whether it was that, how to avoid the same thing again. If you're interested in the issues of chemistry of poison, what is poison to whom and so on, you can go into that in due course. First of all, take it out. What you have got to take out, pluck out, is all attachment, of any kind, to anything, whatever."

Me   How do you do that?

RDL   Take it out! There are sutras and manuals. Follow the time-honored Eightfold Path.

When I pressed Laing for details he breezily told me to look it up. I did and found the following list which is available in almost all books on Buddhism:

1. right views

2. right aspirations

3. right speech

4. right behavior

5. right livelihood

6. right effort

7. right thoughts

8. right contemplation

Although it seems abstract as a list, I did give it considerable attention by reading about it in several books on Buddhism and bringing befitting questions to bear on my own eightfold path.

I had never quite resolved my feelings about my family and had tried to turn off my thinking about them, encapsulating them as a painful node of experience. I therefore thought I might benefit from some right contemplation about them. After considerable time had passed I began by writing my memories of my family in a notebook as part of the assignment of writing down my own story. In retrospect I could see the patterns that formed me, the recapitulations, the working through of guilt, the themes of expiation and redemption, and finally the two-sided danger and opportunity that was emerging with Laing. And thus I will share with you my salutary project:

My Story

The enduring search for love and understanding that has carried me to R.D. Laing began with the drama of my family. They played rough....

Once upon a time before dentists wore masks and color movies were only seen in theaters, I lived with my father and mother in a three-room apartment in Brooklyn.

For my first seven and a half years I flourished in the singular limelight of my parent's attention. My schoolteacher mother, Edith Ottenstein, suspended her proudly won teaching career to provide me with the constancy of care that she thought was my birthright. I wonder if my mother got her just rewards. As the beneficiary of bounteous parental attention I spoke at six months, calling for Da Da, and by one year was allegedly speaking in full sentences, but could not walk. My father, Frank Ottenstein, was a businessman. He took me with him on weekend walks to my mother's neighborhood relatives as soon as I was ambulatory. I adored him and he was endlessly interested in my questions and accomplishments. While we happily strolled down Brooklyn's Church Avenue hand in hand, licking our vanilla Mellorolls, my mother was visiting her own mother and sister across the street. This arrangement was quite congenial to all of them — or so it appeared.

I was enrolled in kindergarten at four, wailing in protest, and progressed through grade school, distinguished only for an original prize-winning story that I told in a contest in the sixth grade. It was a take-off on the tale of Frankenstein that I discreetly linked to my circumstances in what my therapist, 30 years later, sardonically referred to as "the Ottenstein household" by juxtaposing the characters in my family with the characters in the story.

Frank Ottenstein, the protagonist in the fictional drama, bore the name of my real father, with whom I identified. In the tale, Frank was a child genius with a scientific bent. His story-mother, who bore a singular resemblance to my own real-life mother, had only a superficial appreciation of his extraordinary talents. In an attempt to win the approval of her neighbor, Frank's mother planned to demonstrate her four-year-old son's precociousness by having him cross the street on his own. Although far superior evidence of his accomplishments was readily available, this was the fictional Mrs. Ottenstein's method of choice.

In her haste to begin the demonstration, she accidentally shoved Frank in front of a passing car which ran him down, crushing his skull — demonstrating how dangerous lack of proper appreciation can be.

A great, but reclusive, scientist who had befriended and worked with the gifted young boy happened to be at the scene of the accident. He quickly scooped up the bloody boy in his arms and ran to his nearby laboratory to try out a chemical antidote that he had been working on to release super powers. Alas, it didn't work, and poor Frank was buried at the age of four, his genius left dormant in the earth.

The story continues: Before long, the earth around the grave turned red, as if there had been a strong chemical reaction. The old scientist noted this and spent time investigating. One day the discolored earth around the grave cracked open:

Young Frank emerged, larger than life and fully imbued with super powers. In a fury, he proceeded to strangle his old scientist-friend who was out and about in the graveyard. A distant bystander, who witnessed this, heard only part of the scientist's half-muffled cry, "It's Frank Ottenstein." He heard, "Its Frank — instein," and that's how the myth of the monster Frankinstein was born.

For this tale I won a cowboy hat that was too small for my head. The theme embodied in the saga — of my under-appreciated sensibilities — took its own tortuous route in my real family.

When I was about seven and a half years old my mother solicitously came to my bedside at night and asked me if I wanted a baby brother or sister or a dog. Without hesitation I chose the dog, but *my mother was in her ninth month of pregnancy and the die was already cast.*

Jay was born. The limelight would no longer be my own. I can still remember when my brother was brought home from the hospital, with a temporarily mottled forehead, sporting a white knitted garment. The first thing I gave him was a yellow telephone rattle that he grasped with his tiny hand. My mother warned me not to touch him, as if he was a loaded bomb about to go off, but this attitude soon gave way to an active expectation that I should help with the care of Jay. Furthermore, I was presented with my first doll carriage and a life-size boy doll about this time. Somehow I got the message, and my brother became my own.

My father's fascination with me did not extend to my brother. His relationship with his wife worsened, and they even stopped the perfunctory good-bye kiss they used to exchange when he went to work. I don't remember ever seeing them kiss again after Jay was born.

My mother became obsessed with her cute little boy, affectionately known as Jay-Z-Boy. As my father withdrew, my mother needed my assistance with Jay at every turn. I kept a log of Jay's accomplishments from his first grasp of the telephone rattle to the date the scab finally fell off his vaccination (authenticated by the discarded scab glued on the appropriate page in my log book). Jay's toilet training was laboriously documented as well. His development did not follow the normal course. Everything took longer than was expected, but we were expected not to mention this. He did not play with the other children in kindergarten, and I expected my own friends to fill the gap.

When Jay was a seven year old camper and I was fourteen and a junior counselor at camp, my primary mission was to watch my little brother. I loved him. He needed me. It was a simple equation.

Take care of your brother *was so ingrained in my early training that I might well have worn it as an emblem on a crest ring. I cried with unfamiliar ecstasy when the other boys in Jay's camp group carried him above their shoulders in celebration of his hitting a decisive* *home run in the last inning, with the bases loaded. It was an isolated instance – the home run, that is. By 13 Jay would only do his homework with my help. I was given my own TV as compensation for my nightly attentions to him.*

As I assumed more parental responsibilities, I became increasingly important to the functioning of the family. My mother paradoxically spared me from the routine household chores often taken on by youngsters in homes with working parents. I offered moral support and helped maintain my brother's appearance of normalcy. No one had yet made clear what was really wrong with Jay, but he seemed to require more and more special attention.

While Jay was the rewarding focus of much of my youthful attention, he was not the only passion of my childhood.

On my eleventh birthday, my family moved from their one-bedroom Brooklyn apartment to a prototypical two-bedroom brick home in Floral Park, Long Island, complete with an additional basement apartment which was used as a work and play area for the family. Although I was initially housed in the same bedroom as my brother, before long my parents hired a carpenter to begin work on the finished attic where I was to live for the next nine years. This knotty-pine walled two-room suite was custom designed, with an individually designed desk, and built-in dresser and shelves and a large walk-in closet that lit up when the door opened, a standard of luxury that I had never before experienced. One attic room looked out on a carefully tended backyard dominated by a large graceful dogwood tree, and it was designated as my room. It was decorated with custom-made, matching pink corduroy spread, curtains, and vanity skirt that I selected. The second attic room, with its built-in desk and shelves, was to be my father's den. And thus we were to share the attic floor. In reality, my father rarely came upstairs.

The attic belonged to me, and there I read insatiably, compulsively keeping a list of every book that I devoured. I had a sense of myself as destined for some extraordinary purpose and wanted to make sure that any future biographers would be afforded complete documentation, just in case I turned out to be right. At 16, I became captivated by Freud and dreamed of being a great psychologist, unveiling secrets and facilitating miraculous cures, while charging 25 dollars per hour, a very respectable sum in 1960. My father was sure I could do this. Ever receptive, he frequently shared books or records with me, Bertrand Russell, I.F. Stone, and Beethoven. Although he had a short formal education, he lost himself in The Nation and The New Republic, emerging to send an occasional check for liberal causes to Eleanor Roosevelt in spite of his wife's protests that she would rather use the money for a new dress. Adrift in the world of ideas, Frank Ottenstein shared his treasury of thinkers only with me, his receptive daughter, but rarely talked about his work.

When his wife addressed him, he often had to reorient himself as if he was just returning from Mars, and would inevitably say "where, what, when? " no matter what she had said to him. Understandably, his wife found this somewhat disconcerting. While my father's physical self sat nightly in his green Barcalounger and appeared at dinner armed with a newspaper, as far as I could discern my father's sentient self had left his wife's side many years before, if it had ever been there at all. In a rare attempt to elucidate this state of affairs my father told me that my mother had refused to put her money together with his in a joint account when he went into the Army during World War II. Since he did support her for the rest of his life without requiring that she contribute her income from teaching, I marveled at the extent of his distrust. My mother had equally embarrassing stories of his neglect to tell.

Not interested in my dreams of future greatness, my mother would often short-circuit what I considered to be the most engrossing conversations with my father, advising me to go upstairs to bed. She wished I would depart, appropriately married to a Jewish doctor, giving her back the attention of her husband and certifying her as successful mother at the same time. Her cause wasn't without merit.

As I approached 17, Jerry, an ROTC-soldier-engineering student, took a romantic interest in me. My mother, aglow with enthusiasm, became my staunch ally in buying dating outfits. After a stressful day teaching increasingly rebellious classes, she would selflessly hem my dresses and skirts in the service of increasing her eligible daughter's allure to the waiting world of Jewish would-be-professional boys. My mother was so overjoyed by Jerry's promising attentions that she failed to notice my lack of reciprocity. During our tearful breakup scene which took place in the privacy of the attic den, my mother cheerfully burst in with an encouraging bowl of fruit; her timing was ever impeccable.

My father was less enthusiastic about my interest in boys. He kept the phone number of every date in his top drawer. He would wait up for me, and if I had not returned by eleven, he felt free to call up. This vigil was kept up until I finally left for graduate school at 20. But while living in Floral Park, I eagerly reported to my parents, anxious to share the delights of the Jewish-doctor boyfriend I adored from ages 18 to 21. This reporting function coupled with a dull fear of being thought of as a loose woman, kept me relatively innocent until I had moved out of their Long Island home.

Before that, at 18, overriding my father's objections, I went on a supervised 10-week trip to Europe. Although I had saved money working as a waitress the previous summer to finance this adventure, my delighted mother added 300 dollars for exotic purchases for me, herself, and her sister and mother who were still in Brooklyn. No one in my family had ever been to Europe. Surely this trip would increase my stock in trade. Reluctantly, my father joined in, contributing a travel iron as a token of his hesitant approval.

I can still see his sad hazel eyes watching fatalistically as I boarded the plane. Although his eyes still spoke to me until his death years later, I imagine, now, that it was at this point that his voice stopped, his vital voice, that is. My father was becoming a sad and disappointing man, rather than the heroic supporter he had been in my quest for life.

While abroad I received numerous newsy letters from my mother and even a few from 11 year-old Jay, but there was curiously nothing from my father. Europe's wonders, the David and the

Sistine Chapel, the Left Bank of Paris, the Van Goghs in Holland, the fields of England, and even the beer halls in Germany were thrilling to me. I exhaustively shopped through the then-low-priced and kaleidoscopic markets of 13 European countries. At the end of this adventure I touched down in New York, bursting with gifts and stories to tell. My mother arrived at the airport flanked by my best friend Virginia and Virginia's mother. This entourage was necessary because my mother refused to drive herself around, even though she had a license. My father was curiously absent. Exchanging conspiratorial glances with her procession as they got into Virginia's mother's car, my mother suddenly explained to me that my father had had a lung removed soon after I had left for Europe. Cancer. "He just got home from the hospital today" she added informatively.

When I finally reached home, I could see that the essence of life had largely left my father. He had shrunk and looked frail and afraid. I was assured that his body was on the mend. Arthur Godfrey had had the same operation. He was doing fine. So much for the consequences of leaving home.

Although I resumed my familiar household responsibilities, chauffeuring my mother about, tutoring my reluctant brother, and acting as a general negotiator, my desire to be free grew stronger. I had a mission in that house, but I wanted to follow another path. The vision of my father's haunted eyes did not leave me.

My father ostensibly healed and went back to work, but his schedule seemed coincident with my own. Whether my first class started at 8:00 AM or 10:00 AM, he always drove me and often Virginia as well to Queens College. And when I arrived home, so did he. He never suggested that he was making any special accommodations for my convenience. I knew that he didn't want to miss any time with me and that he always knew I would leave him. I thought that must be the reason my father had such sad eyes. And so, with a real sense of foreboding — what would happen to my family without me? — I left for graduate school to study for a Ph.D. in clinical psychology at the University of Oklahoma. At that time my parents and 13-year-old brother gave appearances of being intact, but I knew their days were numbered. I was convinced that I was the link that held them together. They couldn't talk to each other without my translation. It seemed to me that by leaving the scene I was assuming the responsibility for their consequent demise. "How did you kill them?" an analyst would later ask me. But that's another story.

Impressed with the clarity of J.D. Salinger's fictional Glass family and their bulletin board communications, I also had installed a bulletin board for sage quotes on the back of my attic bedroom door. In preparation for my imminent departure, I had wistfully tacked the Japanese haiku, "Oh, plum tree beside my roof, don't forget to bloom each spring," on the board. Actually, it was a comforting and majestic old dogwood tree that presented us with beautiful white blossoms every spring, but it seemed close enough. After I left, I never saw that dogwood bloom again.

For a few months I enjoyed a refreshingly happy and carefree time in graduate school, reading voraciously and riding around the red-earthed Oklahoma countryside on my Moped. In 1964 a woman on a motorcycle, even one as small as a Moped, was a rare occurrence and that, coupled with the fact that I was then the only woman in the clinical psychology program, afforded me enormous attention and freedom compared to my days at the home-based, mostly female Queens College from whence I came.

This idyllic scene was instantly shattered when I received a call from a paternal uncle: "Your father has only two weeks to live. He has a brain tumor. He can say only your name." My mother had evidently attempted to protect me from the demands of this situation by informing me only of less extreme occurrences such as an invented minor stroke, without any mention of a recurring cancer. Nevertheless, the next day I got on a plane to New York, never to return to Oklahoma.

The horrible disorienting weeks that followed were only the beginning of my family's tortured demise. My father did not actually die for five years; he soon regained enough mastery to insure that his wife was not permitted to visit him. The doctors agreed that she *was a very neurotic woman, too hysterical and upsetting for him to deal with. No one with the power to change things suggested that my father's tumor might have been causing his erratic behavior. After years of cold warfare, he now wanted a divorce. I was made the official go-between. My brother wanted to stay with me and our father, under my care in the New York hotel my uncle had arranged for, but had to settle for helping me to placate our mother as we moved our ailing father in ambulances from hospital to hospital. Our mother was understandably humiliated and furious. I understood, but compassion came later, much later. To me at 20, the world seemed chaotic and unreal. I longed for the carefree days in Oklahoma where all I had to do was read books, go to class, and ride around the oil-well-studded countryside on my Moped. Somehow, without wanting to, I had become head of the household.*

When I first arrived back in New York, I had helped my distressed mother by complying with her request and convincing her angry and unwilling husband to sign money over to his wife. But after a while I resented my mother's insatiable demands and insensitivity. My father's death-passion to be finally separated from his wife seemed to me, then, to be a final expression of a discord and lack of communion that had always been there lurking beneath a thinly veiled semblance of normalcy. I imagined that he did not want to spend the time remaining to him trapped in a combative relationship. Although I was moved by my father's anguish, I knew that I would bring about an irreparable break between my mother and myself if I went along with his desire to be separate from her. Nevertheless, guided by my youthful perceptions, I felt that my father had really stayed with his wife all those ill-natured years because of his unspoken devotion to me. I therefore imagined that I owed him my exclusive loyalty in his last days, even if it cost me my relationship with my mother. Time eventually took its toll on the crispness of this reasoning. The exact sequence of events during this tumultuous period is too confusing for me to remember even now.

My brother was thrown out of the public junior high school he attended, and a search for appropriate private schools ensued. I was put in charge of that; no one else could handle Jay. I didn't need graduate school to study abnormal psychology. I had my own case study at hand.

For weeks or months I spent my time almost exclusively on a cancer ward with my slowly recovering father. Our days were filled with radiation and chemotherapy. The doctors finally banned my increasingly hysterical mother from the hospital, because they determined that she was detrimental to her husband's health. My father's brother and sisters, relieved to have me serving as his constant companion, visited him in the hospital. They called me regularly and ceremoniously for reports of his progress and treated me with uncommon regard. Following our tradition of mutual study, I brought my father a book about dying. He showed no interest.

Instead, after the immediate life-and-death crisis had passed, he regained his speech and much of his strength. I took incompletes in my Oklahoma courses. Using my government-sponsored school loan, I paid the rent due to my two Oklahoma roommates for the remainder of the term and moved into a New York hotel with my recovering father. As his caretaker, I provided meals which bore evidence of my lack of experience as a cook — overdone French toast and omelets — and carted him about to doctors. My estranged and strained mother unjustly accused me of staying with my father for his money. She called her ailing husband nightly, telling him to come home. At that time I couldn't stand her. My friends were away at graduate schools. Lonely and upset, I ate excessively to comfort myself.

After a number of dreary weeks of this hotel-medical regimen, my father succumbed to my mother's calls and went home to Floral Park, insisting on taking me with him. By this time my mother was so stressed that she had entered a hospital for an exacerbated diabetic condition that now required insulin injections. As a condition of my return to Floral Park, I negotiated what I hoped would be a separate and safe domain for myself, my own basement apartment. I was to have freedom of movement and be able to see whomever I thought appropriate. The basement had a separate entrance and its own kitchen and bathroom. Only my mother's washer and dryer and mangler were down there. When my mother returned from the hospital, she obviously saw no reason to honor an agreement between her rebellious daughter and weakened husband. She had no intention of arranging with me to go down to the basement to use her own washing machine. So off I went, foolishly angry with my father for breaking his promise, after I had sacrificed both my relationship with my mother and my very desirable graduate school arrangements for him. My world was destroyed. I had fallen from the honored position of acting head of household: I became an outcast.

From ages 21 to 22 I lived in about 10 places, from the aforementioned hotels with my father, to the nearby house of a distant cousin (causing my mother and father much additional humiliation), to sharing apartments separately with two friends still in the New York area, to a Richmond Hill furnished attic, and finally to a rent-controlled, three-room garden apartment behind a butcher shop in Jamaica, Queens. I finished my University of Oklahoma course work from New York and in doing so worked on a paper on the psychosomatic aspects of cancer (of which there were many), while at the same time supporting myself with part-time waitress jobs in coffee shops and a bowling alley. I then got a scholarship at The City University of N.Y., with the idea of earning a Masters in the more definitive subject of physiological psychology.

My mother and most of her family never forgave me. My uncle who had empowered me with temporary head-of-household status when I was twenty-one completely lost interest in me.

My brother went from liberal to progressive private schools, doing summer stints consecutively as a patient in a mental hospital and then an inmate in the Brooklyn House of Detention for selling pot to a police officer in plain clothes, only to return again to Floral Park. His cute crew-cut and innocent face belied his onerous behavior. Jay had robbed our home. He and his so-called friends helped themselves to all of my mother's jewelry but left behind the gold charm bracelet that was given to me on my sixteenth birthday and the few other valuables that were mine. He had a strange way of saying "I love you." On another occasion Jay and his pals took my ailing father's one remaining treasure, his collection of full-color feature films that he had arduously amassed by splicing together remnants of Twentieth Century Fox hits, like The Ten Commandments, for what was then unprecedented home viewing. We were not a highly gregarious family and these rare social events with my father at the helm as projectionist and my mother serving popcorn to the neighbors in the family room of our finished basement put us on the map in Floral Park. On several occasions my best friend Virginia's parents made rare neighborly visits to our house for these events.

The previously fully stocked film racks which had lined the walls of the basement projection room looked ominously forlorn framing the unused ping-pong table that now stood in the center of the room. After my departure our 3-bedroom Floral Park home had turned into a house of horrors. Years later, even when other aspects of my life were rewarding, just the thought of my family's tumultuous downfall entrapped me in a miasma of negativity and doom.

Without me to attend to him, Jay grew more unruly, first flunking out of junior high school because he had stopped trying and then prematurely leaving two private high schools. During this time Jay was also submitted to a summer stay at a plush Long Island mental hospital. Shock was ubiquitously offered up as the treatment; the choice was between electric or insulin – a very unappealing menu. I was appalled at the possibility of shock being given to my teenage brother and used all of my persuasive powers to convince my mother not to sign the necessary release. She was angry – she couldn't control Jay – the doctors had told her that shock was the only path to take. I fantasized running away with Jay and masterminding an escape which would leave us living anonymously as futilely hunted outlaws. They would have come after me. Jay was a minor.

I didn't spring him. My mother signed the permission papers. Jay had the treatment. He cut his hair. His rebellious spirit was quieted – like a gelding he had temporarily lost his prance.

Inside me a door closed on my mother: I viewed unsolicited shock as an instrument of torture. After that summer, when Jay was back, a short-haired student in a private high school exhibiting anew his failure to adjust to expectations, I wanted to take him with me. Although this would not have been an ideal arrangement, I think we could have managed, but that was one release my mother would not sign. Jay continued to self-destruct.

Adrift in a cold sea of familial isolation, at age 22, I was taken with a former classmate, Charlie, a turtle-necked intellectual. Charlie's warmth, poetry, and attention were a lighthouse in the storm. He listened to my stories with compassion and told me his own. I was romanced by his classical music and radical philosophies. He held me and told me poignant stories of the little match girl. On our fateful first date he belatedly returned the library card which he had borrowed from me, presented me with a book on Buddhism, and moved in to my newly acquired rent controlled apartment in Jamaica behind a kosher butcher shop and directly over the subway. Seizing the moment, his mother sent his books over soon after. He introduced me to shared familiarity for the first time and accepted my wayward brother Jay, for which I was eternally grateful. Jay had a key to our Jamaica apartment because I wanted him to have it as a safe place and he was always welcome.

In turn I introduced Charlie to earning a living and other useful skills. We loved each other after a fashion, and I began to be restored. After a few months, the widowed "butcheress-landlady" objected to our living in sin. Since I had lived in 10 places the year before, I did not want to leave our garden apartment which by now also harbored a pet dog. In self-defense we got married. It seemed to be a fair exchange, but for my parents it was the final defeat. Charlie was neither Jewish nor a doctor; he had a crippled arm and had never worked at a regular job. Furthermore he had dropped out of school and just hung around the laboratory proselytizing rebellious political dogma. By the time we got married he had progressed to selling light bulbs over the phone. My father thought that Charlie was only good for sweeping around the house. Actually, I thought that Charlie saved me.

On the rare occasions when I saw my parents again, I made sure that Charlie was always with me.

Under the yoke of emotional dèpendency, I focused on teaching Charlie to drive a car, to hold on to his wallet — a feat he had been previously unable to achieve — now accomplished by chaining it to his belt and to get a succession of increasingly appropriate jobs. I subsequently became disenchanted with graduate school, then did a stint as a case worker, followed by one as a computer programmer/analyst, and culminated this search by engaging in a more long-lasting and creative career as an independent recruiter of computer professionals. Charlie finished college with honors and followed my career path up to the programmer/analyst part. I felt very useful and appreciated as his guide, but I found out that being useful was not enough — a truth I had suspected.

I spent several years regretting my hasty commitment and gaining weight in an attempt to restore my equilibrium. I distracted myself with ice cream, Tarzan books, and an unusual assortment of pets which had grown to include a Capuchin monkey, two dogs, one cat, and a turtle. I drove around New York on my red Yamaha motorcycle — having upgraded from the Moped — with a monkey literally on my back. When I stopped for traffic lights nearby motorists were surprised by the small monkey hands appearing from under my helmet grasping my face mask in an affectionate hug. The monkey helped, but I was ambitious for more. Therapy ultimately reversed the process and I found myself with an irrepressible urge to be light, free, and inspired. Although this may sound like the would-be star of a liberated ladies cigarette ad, my attitude was actually the result of effort and determination. I persisted, trying diverse methods to pull myself out of the quagmire.

My mother decanted my father into a remote New Jersey nursing home not long after he was back in Floral Park. Whenever Charlie and I visited him on my motorcycle in the bowels of New Jersey, he would ask me to take him home. Although his requests tore at me, I did not. He died there several years later at 65.

As if on a diabolical schedule, my mother suddenly died five years after that from diabetic complications, when she was 65. She was living with Jay at the time — he had just turned 21 — in their Floral Park home. By then, Jay was living a painful life, anesthetized by heroin and supported as ever by his mother. She was completely focused on him, still thinking of him as Jay-Z-Boy. She had never visited me after my marriage.

On her gravestone, in a Jewish cemetery, I had inscribed a Latin saying by Saint Augustine, "Legem non habet necessitas." None of the mourners knew Latin, but my mother had studied it in school. It means, necessity knows no law. Recently I have been wondering whether this might be an appropriate epitaph for myself, but at the time it was the most generous tribute I could come up with for my mother.

In spite of my strained relationship with my mother, her death left me morbidly depressed. I found it difficult to get up in the morning, and I returned calls left on my answering machine days later, if at all. Somewhere during this period I lost the incentive to make money, but strangely my recruiting business became more profitable. I was becoming more reflective and more sensitive to those around me. Perhaps my clients sensed that? For the most part, they developed a remarkable loyalty to me, and the placement of professional computer people supported me, in style, with relatively little effort for the next 10 years!

My feelings for Charlie became more maternal than matrimonial, and I was working toward an amicable divorce. I had hoped we would remain loving friends. Charlie seemed reluctant to actuate our divorce plans, however, and alternated between writing me love poems, drinking, and knocking me around. We were both in therapy. Charlie would have held on, but I forced the issue and found myself thin, newly alive, alone, and divorced in New York City.

When my mother died, Jay, as if prompted by her benevolence, used the money she had left in trust for him to buy drugs. The next four years were a series of disasters for him. The high point was provided by a Long Island Mafia chief who had Jay taking care of a disabled relative who could not speak. The Mafia did not approve of drugs. Jay would solicitously put this isolated man on the phone when he called me, so that I could talk to him. But the silent man died, ending Jay's role.

My father's sister and brother-in-law also tried to help by hiring Jay to work for them, but all attempts failed. Jay called me once, high on angel dust, and told me that he wasn't destined to live out a full-length life. During this telephone conversation he also told me that I had been better to him than anyone else had. He ended his life in a furnished room in Floral Park, one block from our prototypical brick home. He and Elvis Presley died of an overdose of an assortment of drugs on the same summer day.

By the time Jay died at 25, he had been the unfortunate victim of multifarious misfortunes: maternal overprotection and indulgence, paternal disinterest and illness, sisterly abandonment, shock treatment in a mental hospital, a short stint in the Brooklyn House of Detention, babysitter for the Mafia, and more.

Was Jay just angry, disturbed, unbalanced, or biochemically off? Whatever he was, he was also my own. He went straight to my heart. The link between us was never fully severed and like him, Laing, too, is a part of me now.

After having been spurned by my family, married to Charlie for seven years, in therapy for four years, and divorced (we never saw each other again), I attempted to embody a continuation of this regenerative growth theme by planting a real plum tree on the penthouse roof of the apartment to which I had moved in my thirtieth year. When the last of my family, my brother, died at twenty-five, the plum tree, as if on cue, died as well. After my divorce and the aforementioned serial deaths I just didn't have the energy to give the plum tree enough water to sustain life, and the New York City winds and heat finished it off. As I had feared, my immediate biological family had consumed themselves prematurely, leaving me in their wake, the sole survivor, to live out the repercussions. My father, mother, and brother had fallen like dominoes in series, each providing a successor with the means for his own demise. Between 1969 and 1977, Edith, Frank and Jay Ottenstien had died, separately and alone. I wanted to live.

When I got my strength back, I chopped the dead plum tree down with an ax and burnt it, Indian-like, in my fireplace, hoping for a quick symbolic resolution. It took more time though. The denouement of my resolution took the path of a search, guided by reason and fueled by passion. Although I was isolated and hungry, weighing in momentarily at only 110 pounds, my roots were good. I reasoned that it was only a matter of time and attending to the right variables (loving service and attention) before I was restored.

By 1977 when Jay died, I had developed an operating plan to deal with losses that magically lifted me out of the quagmire of despair, giving me something to do and at the same time setting the stage for a more appropriate, healing and timely expression of grief. There's no sense in crying to yourself while everything around you goes down the drain. In the right circumstances grief can be cathartic and a natural part of life, rather than merely a lonely and painful disaster.

My operating plan to deal with losses covered the loss of treasured things as well as people. My policy was simple, and perhaps awful-sounding: **Replace the loss with something or someone better. Also in the case of the loss of a loved person, one was to take something good from him or her, avoid looking backwards, and move on to the task of replacement, using all the intelligence and diligence one could muster. This is to be regarded as a time-limited operation: There's no point in going on forever without at least a quantum of love.**

If the loved person had died, he was in a sense to be incorporated and thereby made immortal. So I looked for good qualities of the departed to make my own. This procedure is difficult to communicate to the uninitiated (those who are unacquainted with sudden sweeping changes in their support systems). It has a macabre aspect to all but concentration camp survivors. The survivors I've met thought it was quite admirable.

My compensation system began when my father died in 1969.

After my messy divorce, I found myself alone with a successful business, but without a cast of friends and family. I studied various systems of psychotherapy, training myself for the Herculean mission before me. Alternating between fear and optimism, I made a list of the cast I wanted to play with, drawing from the most engaging characters of my past, regardless of my importance to them. Since I had no one, I reasoned that I might as well aim for the best.

I headed this magical list with Bill Reynolds, a strikingly handsome, brainy, and much-fantasized-about psychology professor/attorney whom I had last seen a decade earlier at Queens College. I had shared my intoxicating fantasies about Bill Reynolds with my girlfriends who also sat admiringly in the first row of his various psychology classes.

I made a game plan, and head-hunter-style, customized my approach to attract him. At this time I was strong and tan and shapely from sunning myself in my terrace hammock and working out in my green leotard among the flowers with a private instructor on the gymnastic rings I had had mounted there. I had long shiny brown hair and dark dancing eyes. "Let me pretend that I am the therapist and you are the patient," I told the still-beautiful Dr. Reynolds. He barely recognized me after 10 years of absence, but his curiosity, twinkling in his baby blue eyes, was aroused. Later, at his invitation, I showed him my ground rules, the same 22 steps specified in this book, the same procedures I used to reach R.D. Laing and other people who turned out to be vital to me. Professor Reynolds went for it. Dr. Laing did, too. It's a pretty good plan if attracting love is one of your goals.

It was then that I picked up the long-abandoned intellectual studies that I had begun with my father. Casting aside my Tarzan books so useful in my less active period when they carried me above it all, as I flew through the trees with my imaginary hero, Tarzan, lightening many uninspired days, I now set off on my own mythical journey, studying energetically to find my power.

My love for my father was to be, in a sense, resurrected in the people who would come to share this mythical quest with me.

My unwitting search to fill my mother's place was less clear than my attempts to replace my father, just as my relationship with her was more ambiguous. My feelings for her were fraught with contradictions.

Although I still resented her, I was also grateful to her for giving me life and taking care of me. I remembered too the ways she had loved me in my youth: correcting my spelling, sometimes with the added tutorial of Latin roots, and laying out travel directions for me each time I went to an unfamiliar place. She must have learned this from her substitute teaching days when she had to travel around the City from school to school. After her death I learned to fly a plane — and used a map to chart the trip in excruciating detail, including the recording of anticipated visual cues and local radio tower frequencies. I began to assume the responsibility for knowing how to get where I wanted to go. My spelling, as a result of concerted effort, also improved dramatically, but it was not until the advent of the computerized spell-checker that is part of my word-processing program that I was home-free. Sometimes when I look up a word I can still hear her voice giving the Latin roots. She was a good teacher.

When it came to my brother's death in 1977, I was at temporary loss to find a token quality to emulate and I chose his nose, which was straight and beautifully proportioned. Don't laugh yet. Let me explain.

I had been very fortunate to find a brilliant and generous man called Richard who loved, accepted, and needed me in his own customized intentional family constellation. He had proudly brought me to his senior partner, Arthur, a scholarly, gifted, ruthless, and ambitious self-made-millionaire-financier. After a convivial evening in which we all talked and Arthur probed my knowledge of economic models (enhanced by my economist friend, Bill, who had loved and sustained me through difficult times), Arthur generously suggested to Richard that he fix my nose, which had been broken for as long as I could remember. In private Richard made me this most unusual offer. Because I regarded myself as attractive and in good shape at this time, I took Richard's offer as a compliment. My nose had been broken at some unspecified time without notice when I was a child. I was used to it, but I regarded Author's suggestion that Richard invest in me in this fashion as a seal of approval from a very shrewd investor and as an act of love from Richard. After all why pay for nose jobs on people who are not at least in some way your own? I now felt that I belonged to Richard, and he acted that way as well. Nevertheless, I said "no, thank you" only because I was afraid of hospitals. I had never been in one except to be born. That event had resulted in a two-week stay in a plastic box for premies. (My birth weight was just over four pounds). I wasn't anxious to go back again.

Jay's death had marked the final break between myself and most of my family. (Only my mother's sister, Mary, remained in touch with me and eventually came to visit me with her friend Sylvia.) In a well-intentioned attempt to create a meaningful funeral for my brother, after he died drugged and alone in a furnished room one block from our former home in Floral Park, I wanted to gather all those who knew him in my apartment in New York and have those who wished say something in remembrance. I thought perhaps we would all exchange with each other some of the energy we had invested in him. This concept was far too alien for all but my father's brother Jules, who did show up along with Richard's family. My brother's death knell sounded the changing of the guard. Richard's family became my own, complete with children and mother. I now had a place in the world. My historical family made their own funeral for Jay, one which complied with convention and had meaning to them, but left me out. I changed my name to Russell, marking my departure from my family and symbolically attaching myself to Bertrand Russell who was not around to object.

And now I'll tell you the culmination of the nose story: Jay had a beautiful aquiline nose. When I went to identify his body his face looked finally serene and beautiful. I knew what people mean when *they repeat the seemingly nonsensical phrase, "He was finally at peace."*

Eventually I sent myself to a doctor recommended by Arthur and had the dreaded nose surgery, buttressing myself against the fear of being inadvertently done in by the hospital by prearranging a vigil of visitors who arrived every hour or two. So I have Jay and the doctor and Arthur to thank for my happily straightened nose. I also have Jay to thank for teaching me a great deal about how to love. You see, he did love me. He trusted me. He needed me. He gave to me. When all the world was dark for him, he still had the strength to tell me I was O.K. He still loved me, even though I left him there in the desert of Floral Park when he was only thirteen.

* * *

Writing this essay helped me to integrate my complex feelings about Jay, and after completing it I felt more serene.

My project with Laing reveals this sort of motivation to change in me but not in Laing. I was unyielding in my insistence that he change. Had I been smarter, I might have given up my efforts to change him and concentrated, instead, on using my love for him and my desire to serve him to change myself. I did, however, find enough inspiration in working with Laing to go beyond my limits of commitment and motivation to increase my options for a fuller, more intimate life.

It is easy to see how I had set myself up with Laing for a potential repetition of my past expulsions from my family. Were these experiences what Laing had referred to when he had so insightfully told me, "When we cry for others we cry for ourselves," the very first time he approached me after I had tearfully witnessed the expulsion scene of the conference organizers in Spain?

I was in dangerous territory, and sought the structure of a workable system with Laing to stabilize my highly charged emotional situation and to complete our book project successfully.

It was still 1981, and motivated by my desire to change I was trying to see my patterns more clearly. Old memories that had long been buried were now being churned up and subtly reframed. My perspective was expanding, and I found myself more able to examine my possible motives for the embarassing tenacity with which I seemed to hold on to my much talked about, extra thirty-five pounds.

Laing also began to show interest in my motives and before long I found myself rather frighteningly under the lazer beam of his scrutiny.

CHAPTER SEVEN

Here's Looking At You, Kid

"Sit down before fact, as a little child, be prepared to give up every preconceived notion, follow humbly wherever and whatever abysses nature leads or you will learn nothing."

Thomas Huxley

Laing and I searched for quite a while before we found a workable structure for our project together. During our initial foraging for something congenial to do together we focused on one of my presenting complaints, which was my desire to weigh less.

Me   If you could motivate me from a book to go out and pick somebody, if you could induce me to commit myself, and do whatever it was that worked, how would you do it? Now, you wouldn't set up a rigid system that seems inappropriate to you, where I would have to make eye contact when it didn't feel natural to make eye contact or where I would have to sit and listen to somebody when actually I couldn't care less.

What would you set up? How could *you* encourage some-body? What would do it for you? What's your number?

RDL   Well, take the word "love," for instance. The word "love" as it appears in the Old Testament. "Love thy neighbor as thyself" doesn't mean love Tom, Dick and Harry. *(Both laugh.)* <u>Who</u> is thy neighbor?

I seized the moment, taking this rhetorical question as a tangential invitation to see myself in the light of Laing's attention. Laing at last gave his attention to my desire to change.

Me   As for <u>me</u>, I'm overweight. I'd like to change that.

RDL   What do you mean by "overweight"?

Me   I mean I don't like myself because I weigh too much.

RDL   You mean when you look in the mirror?

Me   Yes, when I look in the mirror. Not because someone told me. I used to be thirty-five pounds lighter, and I felt good.

RDL   Didn't someone tell you what you're supposed to like when you look in the mirror?

Me   I looked a lot better thirty-five pounds lighter. I don't need anybody to tell me. When I walked around in a bikini I felt like dynamite. I don't do that now. I'm too fat. Thirty-five pounds lighter, that's what I want to be.

RDL   You don't want to be as sexually attractive as you <u>might</u> be?

Me   Yes. A lot of things start to fall apart when I get to be more sexually attractive.

RDL   What do you mean?

Me   Because I'm very free, I can do as I please. I have nobody to check in with. Look, you have a long-term marriage. No matter what you do, you know, more or less, what you are coming home to. I mean, if I'm free, I'm subject to every son-of-a-bitch who's walking around. I'm turned on by brilliant people. It doesn't matter whether they are nice or not. If I like someone a lot, I might want to go to bed with him.

RDL   So why don't you take your pick?

Me   Well, where I can, I do take my pick—but I don't always get everybody I want.

RDL   If you took the thirty-five pounds off, you'd get a wider pick.

Me   (Laughing) I know I can get a wider pick, but then I have to deal with them.

RDL   Why don't you enjoy that? Why is that a problem? (Making penetrating eye contact.)

Me   I'm afraid they might hurt me.

RDL   How can they hurt you? If you can always say "no" whenever you feel like it...

Me   Well, if I can say "no" whenever I feel like it, it couldn't go any further than I wanted I guess. (Hesitantly)

RDL   That's right. O.K., so there's no problem so far, is there?

Me   Not that way. But going through with a relationship is another thing.

RDL   You're talking about pain. You don't want to be hurt. You've been hurt before. You don't want to be hurt again. It's very easy to get hurt. You've got to be a real toughie if you're in for that sort of thing, if you're out and about, hacking it out, sexually. I mean there is **real love.** Thank God for human love, as Saint Benedict is said to have said, it is the nearest touch humanity has to divine love.

Thank God for human love whichever way it comes, wherever, whenever one finds it, sexual or not.

Me   Absolutely, it's the best there is.

RDL   And people who don't realize <u>that</u>, don't realize that this kind of sexual love involves a lot of pain, terrible mangles, terrible agony.

Me   Let's say I fall in love, and I am sexually attracted by falling in love. I get into a thing of "serving men." And then it's like I'm gone, you know?

Freedom is very important to me, but it's not sufficient. I really do what I please. I'm proud of that, and I have a lot of good times, but my life is not rich enough. I want to be in love with someone, and yet I want, still, to stay my own person, pursue my own pursuits. And I want to have a baby. I don't know how to do all that.

(RDL laughs and subsequently I do, too.)

RDL   If you lost thirty-five pounds, you've got to pick who you're prepared to let yourself into <u>that</u> baby number with.

Me   Yes. (More mutual laughing.)

RDL   And if the sort of person you <u>want</u> is the sort of person who obviously wants you thirty-five pounds less than you are—?

Me   Absolutely! I hope so.

RDL   So you've got to take the thirty-five pounds off. It changes your mind.

He was moving closer, looking directly at me, and speaking emphatically.

Me   Yes, yes. It changes everything. It's just like being rich! (Laughs.)

RDL   **You've got to take the plunge. Just do it.**

Riding high on Laing's focused attention, I tried to link our purposes. I wanted to link my motivation to fight my self-created dragons to his motivation to fight what I thought were his obstacles to a profitable best seller. This attempt, as usual, triggered a round of heated denials:

Me Just do it. Making money is really just writing something people want. It's the same thing. Take the plunge. It's so easy to say.

RDL It's completely different.

Me Oh, no, it's not, it's not. There are things you have to do. If I eat less and move more, I'm going to weigh less. It's as simple as that.

RDL It's not a correct analogy. It's not proper to compare taking thirty-five pounds off one's weight to writing something other people want.

Me No, it is. If you're the person that has it in you, it's just a different parameter.

RDL It's not on the same dimension. They cross each other in different ways. It's a different sort of thing. It's a different domain.

Me I don't think so. I think that your not automatically having a best seller is the same fat on you as my thirty-five pounds is on me. I absolutely believe that. With your level of consciousness, if you just stay *clear* and address yourself to something important to people and communicate it, that's a best seller. But you've got to be clear and courageous and talking about something universal and participating yourself.

RDL The things I've written for the past ten years are, I think. One thing you can't accuse them of is not being lucid. They've been best sellers in England and in Europe and all over the world, in Japan and Italy. About the only place they've not made money is the United States.

Me But your problem is that you want to make money in the

United States <u>now</u>, and a <u>lot</u> of it.

RDL   You keep on telling me I've got <u>that</u> problem. But that's not <u>my</u> problem. I don't see it as a problem.

Me   It's a task.

RDL   No, it isn't. All I <u>can</u> do is to write the sort of things I'm compelled to write. If, as a bonus, people in the United States buy it, I will bring in more money by writing.

Me   Hmm.

RDL   I mean, I don't see making any change. I've just got to keep on with what I'm doing. I may be changed. I can't change. I'm not going to get pulled away by that consideration (the task of writing a best seller for America) which I never had in the first place.

Me   So then you're saying that the only thing you could do is address yourself to marketing.

RDL   I don't want to address myself to marketing.

Me   Your product is coming out of you. It's intrinsic to you. There's nothing you can change. You write "poetry." You can only write what you're experiencing. You can't write for the marketplace. What you're experiencing is perfect. That's the way it goes. There's nothing you wish to change. That's for other people to do. Poets don't sully themselves in the marketplace. Is that right?

RDL   Yup.

Me   And I think poets who are out there taking their chances, who think like you, can't avoid a best seller. And I think it just reflects your level of participation. It's not a blanket statement, because I'm not trying to dismiss what you do. I just think you need to do more. I guess that doesn't make sense to you because you don't believe it or you're resisting me or both.

RDL   It doesn't have anything to do with what I feel, with what I
        am about. You may **be** right, but it doesn't feel right to me.

Me   If you're doing something that's not adaptive, and the fault
        is not in the stars or in external situations...then I say, let's
        see what the situation is and try a solution, but then you say
        your situation is entirely external, nothing to do with what
        you do.

RDL   No, no, I didn't say that.

Me   Oh, I thought you did.

RDL   I said what I wanted was to continue to live as I do, be as I
        am, and more money to come in. I'm not wasting much time
        dwelling on that want. It's not eating my life away. I've never
        talked about it with anyone, even to this extent. I don't want
        to have to try to change. What would that mean? Be
        different from myself in order to get more money to come
        in?

Me   Well, how else can you get more money?

RDL   That's your problem. A leopard can't change his spots.

        I could be marketed just as I am, as a marketable commodity,
        R.D. Laing, just as I stand. And get more money, more money
        to spend.

*Laing was never prepared to put what I thought were his underlying
problems on the table for comparison with my own. Frustrated in
my attempts at logically linking what I thought were our problems,
I was forced to satisfy part of this desire for mutuality elsewhere.
Laing fueled the furnace of my desire to succeed, but my friends
stoked the fire. When I went back to New York City, eight pounds
lighter, I called all of the people I cared about who had a desire to
lose weight. I tried to harness their motivation to mine, asking them
to be accountable, to agree to checkpoints at which they reviewed
and discussed their mutual progress.*

Although I would have preferred to stay in London and continue to enjoy the benefit of Laing's attention, I was clearly not prepared to abandon my project in protest. I had positioned myself so that there was nowhere to go but to follow a successful goal-oriented path. I felt that I needed cohorts to get over the hump of my food addiction. Periodically I still need the moral support and camraderie of fellow food addicts. This was not difficult to find, since most people suffer from eating more than they should, particularly as they get older. I found no shortage of gratefully motivated friends and acquaintances willing to call in once every week to report their struggles and concerns. And soon I re-discovered an old friend who had been inspired by a book about fasting which I had given him years before and he had lost eighty-five pounds on a liquid protein diet. And so inspiration returned to me. After two months of rather dull protein malts, and one mile a day of swimming, I lost the rest of the thirty-five pounds.

Laing's partnership provided a way of spending high quality, attentive time with another person. His attention, commitment, and good intentions were my allies in the battle against my persistent resistance to taking my own common-sense advice. Dr. Eric Graham Howe, a once-famous British psychologist, wrote in *Cure or Heal?* (1965), "As a psychotherapist, I am sometimes asked, 'If you do not use either knives or drugs, what do you do for your patients that justifies your charging fees?' My answer is a very simple one. It is 'I give them TIME.'...To our more wholesome selves... who are interested in patient healing rather than impatient cure, TIME is our healer."

The partnership plan I had set up in this book was not synonymous either with co-counselling or with the helping dyads which are part of the various anonymous self-help groups, but the increased trust and acceptance born of an honorable partnership still provided substantive benefits in terms of my empowerment.

This method was a special form of self-help, a way of increasing my participation in the world, of being more accountable, real, and trustworthy; of thereby being more valuable, confident, valued, and empowered to **take my own advice.** This is a customized, but universal approach that transcends, but still can affect, anyone's <u>particular</u> self-generated problems.

In my case it gave me the powerful motivation and increased self-respect to want to achieve my goals. *Extra energy to approach life's challenges is often an outgrowth of the process of falling in love. It gives one an added sense of purpose.* Whether Laing did what I advised or not, I imagined that I could still be an instrument for our mutual good.

When we had initially met to explore our project in London, I had told Laing that I wanted to serve him. He smiled devilishly and said, "I might use you a little." With complete sincerity, I replied, "That's what I'm here for."

He never actually did misuse me, although we occasionally colluded together to keep my fantasies growing. I found, paradoxically, that every time I offered my services in Laing's behalf they came right back to me again. I wanted Laing to give up his addictions, but to succeed in our venture I had to relinquish my own.

Usually in the evenings Laing would play his Steinway piano which was located in his beautiful book-lined Victorian room, his parlor. He played with abandon and grace and often guests or family members would sing along. He was never without music for long and said that as a youth he had been told by his teachers that he had perfect pitch. He came from a musical household in Scotland where his father had been the chief organist for the church as well as an engineer. Laing said that his mother sang beautifully until she closed the piano one day in protest against some real or imagined ills and never sang again.

Ronnie seemed to me to be a lot like his mother in this respect, since he would avoid bringing up significant people in his past who had injured him. He shut them out as if they had never existed, but actually they came up often in the form of abstract themes. He prided himself on his capacity for detachment.

One late evening, I remember, it was around midnight, Laing told me that he would like to hear my voice a bit more. He would like to have more of my spirit in the room. I froze. I hadn't sung in a small group since childhood. I was terrified. This was not the first time he had mentioned my unwillingness to sing, but this time he was pressing the point. When we were alone in the room he asked me if anything had happened to make me stop singing. After thinking about it, I nervously told him that the last time I remembered singing in public was in summer camp when I was 11 years old and had been asked to withdraw from the group by the counselor. My singing was not up to par then, and I didn't think it had improved over the years. I didn't have perfect pitch and was not about to give a demonstration. Laing seemed very understanding and said he wouldn't press the point just then. I had never met a more empathetic person when it came to frailties. Nobody had ever asked me about this before. I thought I was in heaven: Laing played the piano like an angel, and he wanted more of my spirit in the room. This was a long way from being potentially banished, which I had been afraid of during our initial encounters in London.

On the next late night musical occasion Ronnie and Leon, his psychiatrist friend, were making music around the piano and drinking wine. They were singing one of Ronnie's poems to the tune of "Daisy, daisy, give me your answer true..." and fully enjoying themselves. I loved being there. Ronnie said that if we hadn't been friends we wouldn't be together like that just then, but I still could not bring myself to sing along above a barely audible whisper, even though I adored Ronnie and really wanted to please him. I had promised myself that I would sing for him sometime, however awful I sounded, but I just couldn't bring myself to do it yet. I wanted time to prepare.

Suddenly Leon and Ronnie left the room conspiratorially. Jutta was asleep. I didn't know what was up, but when they returned, Ronnie said that if I did not sing they would both rape me. I was absolutely silent, but nothing happened. Ah, well....

When I went back to New York I took private singing lessons. I sounded terrible but did find myself constantly singing around the house. I started to record my voice for feedback. No, I didn't become a singing star, but I did spontaneously make up a song and mailed the tape to Ronnie:

> I've been around for thirty-seven years
> Going back and forth from caretaker to tears.
> I've been around for thirty-seven years.
> I've read a lot of books
> and I've shed a lot of tears.
> But nobody has been as clear as you
> Nobody's been as pure as you,
> Nobody's opened up their home to me
> their heart to me, as you have.

The song went on and on for many stanzas singing his praises, and Ronnie had the good taste not to say anything about it, but I knew that he got it, and it is included here so you don't think I just jousted with him all the time. He was really very good to me and I felt blessed. The song on tape was a wonderful release for me, and I finally did sing to his accompaniment. I was very nervous, and it was quite bad, but nothing terrible happened.

I was willing to go to the edge to please Laing. **In therapy the client usually follows a course of resistance and transference. Transference is very much like being in love, only the set, setting, and consequences are presumably different. When one is under the spell of the intensely pleasant illusions of being in love or of positive transference, one will run very hard for the approval of the treasured other. Presumably this is the core of the emotive force that gives people the power to change constructively, to triumph over the self-imposed obstacles that cripple them.**

"The struggle between intellect and instinctual life, between understanding and seeking to act is played out almost exclusively in the phenomena of transference. It is on that field that victory must be won—the victory whose expression is permanent cure of neurosis."

Sigmund Freud, 1912

Laing had me positioned to give up my symptoms, if I was to be successful with him. I was trying to do the same thing for him. My relentless attempts to change Laing were not entirely unrewarded. Months later on his second visit with me in New York City, he told me to have plenty of soda in the house for him, no wine or beer, and he did abstain from drinking alcohol during that visit. He said he felt fragile. Laing's abstention from alcohol did not last much longer than the visit, but I took it as an encouraging sign. Nevertheless, he still did not present any formal symptoms to be cured except the lack of a best seller in America, so my success with R.D. Laing remained to be seen.

CHAPTER EIGHT

The Paradox of Faith

What to Do When You Are Not Ready For A Partner

"Those indeed are conquerors who, as I have now, have conquered the intoxications (the mental intoxications arising from ignorance, sensuality or craving after future life). Evil dispositions have ceased in me; therefore it is I that am conqueror!"

Gautama Buddha

"Religion is not what is grasped by the brain, but a heart grasp."

Mohandas Karamchand Gandhi

There are times when one is not ready to go out and find another to work or play with. Sometimes it is best to keep your own company. When I got back to New York from my work visit with R.D. Laing, before I enlisted the aid of my companions in a dieting and exercise rally, I was unable to take any of my own good advice. Missing the richness of Ronnie's immediate attention, I drowned my sorrows in overeating. The more I ate, the more inactive and frustrated I became. Therefore I decided to try some of the following advice Laing had offered during one of our discussions in London:

RDL   Let me give you a contact with a mental-spiritual tradition, to get your response to this strategy, O.K.?

Me   Sure.

RDL   ***You're in pain. You're in an unsatisfactory state of mind.*** You're confused: all sorts of things are not right. Through this confusion what you realize is this: it's very complex, involving your feelings, your relationships; you are thinking of doing something about it yourself and not asking some other fellow to do it. The essential thing to do is the following: ***Realize that the state of mind you're in can be changed by meditation. Turn your attention away from what you are confused about. Take the simplest object—a dot—and all you do is pay all your attention to that dot. Concentrate on it. That is all. In the course of doing that you will experience various transformations of your mind.*** They are well documented. They are describable to some extent. When you've done that, simplified your mental operations down to one, all attention on one thing, you may start paying bare attention to visual objects, objects of vision, then to the faculties of vision, then through all the senses—what you hear, how you hear, <u>who</u> is hearing, seeing, smelling, touching what. ***Don't try yet to give full bare attention to anything as maddeningly complex as another human being.*** That is a very, very difficult meditational experience. Only after you've got yourself somewhat clear can you move on to human relationships, which are the most complex of the lot. But you can't expect not to get more confused by getting into trying to look into your confusion with the confused state of mind that you're in.

Laing rolled his eyes back into his head for emphasis. Then he picked up the half-filled wine glass that was standing on the piano and smiled at me as I warmly encouraged him to go on.

Me   That's good, yes. It makes a lot of sense. I like that. What's
        the special meditation about feelings?

RDL   Again, just paying bare attention to one's feelings. Don't try
        to start or stop them. *Feelings involve intentions of love
        or hatred.* And all that. This is very deep water.

Me   You're supposed to know yourself before you go out.

RDL   Yes, At least to have clarified one's mind to some extent.
        Some people embark on this particular way, and, by the time
        they die, have not come back again.

*When I returned to New York City, I felt confused and hungry. After
calming down enough to meditate about what was bothering me,
I realized the obvious. I just wanted to be around Laing again,
seeing him every day. He just wanted a book; my presence was
not important to him. I felt needy and therefore not very creative.
Wanting to rise out of the quagmire of my particular muddle, I let
my attention float. The only way I could win was to consider my
good fortune at having the opportunity to serve this gifted man
whom I loved so much and not dwell on those missing aspects of
a relationship with him. If I needed more warmth and companionship, I would get it where it was available and not fruitlessly seek
it where it was not offered.*

"That tender compromise called resignation is only an eloquent
name for the dying down, the wearing thin, of the vital impulse in
us. It is just here that it would seem to be of the utmost importance,
for occidental minds, to shake off the sad, self-satisfied metaphysic
of the Orient where such weary resignation, patronizingly con-
temptuous of what it regards as the mad illusions of youth, prides
itself on its irrefutable wisdom. Far nearer to Nature's secret would
seem to be an attempt to get the two spontaneous reactions, of
gratitude to Life and of defiance to Life, fused in some way in our
solitary contemplations."

                                        John Cowper Powys

Looking In...

Me	I think another way to look at the same thing is that people also have five senses. It's like taking responsibility for yourself as a living organism, being as broad-based as you can. This will maximize your movement, because *if you give yourself some things to do which will "feed" you, you can get closer to the way you want to be by increasing the amount of energy you are going to give out. Because it can't come from nowhere.*
RDL	I think there's a very simple way of acquiring energy in about two minutes.
Me	What is the way? One way is physical. One way to feed yourself is to make your physical environment more responsive. But how are you going to change the emotional end of it?
RDL	*The only change that matters is a change of heart.* A change of this sort can only come about exterior to the soul, it comes about by grace. To translate that into modern terminology, you might say something like—all efforts by the ego to acquire more energy will fail. The only way is by a change of heart. Once that change of heart happens, which only happens by grace, then everything changes.
Me	That sounds like a Catch 22 then.
RDL	Yes, *that's the paradox of faith.*
Me	Let's say you are not in a state of grace, which is most likely, and you don't know what to do. Do you sit around waiting for grace to come? Then, of course, you don't have to read a book about it.
RDL	The first thing you do is pray, and if you are a monk, whether in monk's or businessman's clothing, you do nothing else.

You may do two things. You pray, and you go to such a monk
(whatever sort of dress he or she is wearing), to the nearest
holy man or woman, and ask him or her to respond to your
situation.

Me   So that alleviates it.

(I was thinking, "Isn't that what I did coming to you?")

Suppose you're not a traditionally religious person? How do
you know who to go to? Do you use your own instinct as
to where to go? Do you take stock of your situation realis-
tically?

RDL   I would stand still. If I didn't trust my judgment, I would not
act upon it.

Me   Do you really believe that it's always true that you should
just center yourself? Or do you think there **is** some time
when it is right to act?

RDL   Yes, of course there's a time to act and a time to wait, a time
to go out into relationships and a time to withdraw. That is
exactly Ecclesiastes and the I Ching. There's a time to go out
and a time to go in, a time to retreat and a time to advance.
Maybe we could offer some thoughts that would help
readers to make up their minds if they <u>are</u> making up their
minds. But when it comes to doing something, I must say,
no one can tell you actually.

Me   I think people often don't stop to assess the situation, to
check out what they might want and how to get there. *If
you find someone else can be of help to you, it might be
worthwhile to create some design about that.* Do you ever
try to know people?

RDL   That's a funny question, the way you pose it. I don't often
experience any desire to.

Laing continued to find exceptions to my advice. He always seemed
to focus on the frailty of the human condition and the suffering one

must endure in life. He had said that he had never been personally happy. He seemed to have a profound understanding of human suffering.

However frustrating, he actually was a good antidote to my rampant positivism, and I began to be less thwarted, more compassionate, and enriched by his relentless exceptions. ***Stillness and action are really partners, not contradictions.*** And on we went with his exceptions:

RDL   It's very difficult to issue general edicts like that one that you're using—the best way to care for yourself is to care for others. That might be true sometimes.

Me   Well, that's true. If you take care of the wrong others, you might go down the drain just by dissipating your energies. If you don't take care of anyone, I guess there **are** situations when that's the best.

RDL   You might have broken a leg on a hike, and the best thing you can do is to allow yourself to be taken care of. It would be ridiculous to, as it were, preach to somebody who is intellectually and emotionally disabled for the time being, that the best way to get their act together is to "help other people." It might <u>not</u> be the best.

Me   That's true. The most common reason people go into therapy is that they're demoralized. They have a problem either with love or work. Usually there's not too much else. And you could say the best way is not to take care of someone else again if one is already taking care of someone else. That might **be** the problem. I guess it's the "right" someone else and the "right" kind of care that's important.

RDL   Why not just buy a puppy dog or a cat?

I found Laing difficult: He seemed committed to finding exceptions and objections to my recommendations, instead of taking at least part of the responsibility for coming up with something affirmative and substantive to offer the prospective reader. His protestations were eroding my enthusiasm, but I kept on anyway. Sometimes I wondered what I was doing there in Hampstead with this contrary man, but in my mind the alternatives seemed less appealing. I rationalized, thinking that his style was merely the outgrowth of a defensive posture. And on I went, hoping a more congenial tone would emerge in our discussions:

Me   Maybe you should get a puppy dog or a cat, some people advise that, but if you look at yourself, and there's something more you want, *I think you can increase your chances of getting it by binding with the right person to motivate you in pursuit of what it is you want.*

RDL   The people who one is inclined to give that advice to are very often the very people who feel they can't avail themselves of that advice. Other people are like the grapes of Tantalus. They would love to reach out to another person, and they feel very often they do, and they feel that other people mysteriously withdraw from them and say, "Well, keep on doing so..."

Me   I wouldn't say that.

RDL   Or you say, What's the matter with you?

Me   Yes. Say, "Why are you withdrawing?"

RDL   Yes...and they say, "Well, I wish you could tell me!"

Me   I'd send them out to get some feedback, but before they go out to do anything, I'd tell them to go back and relax and try to get themselves reasonably centered.

RDL   I think the most usual feeling of this kind that I've come across is worse than that, or more difficult to do anything about. It is an initial feeling of really being cut off from other people, so that other people are at the other side of an impassable chasm. Some people feel like this and are not particularly shy. They live among and meet other people, even their nearest and dearest. They get married, have children, and feel this even with their children.

Me   Yes, that's true. Only certain people can avail themselves of the kind of help you can get from a book. Some people can't even get the energy to *read* a book, let alone take advice from it, but books can still be helpful. If you don't have enough energy to relate to <u>some</u> extent to other people—I mean, if you're totally out of contact—I don't think any book is particularly helpful.

RDL   When you use that phrase, "to yourself," what do you mean, "look to"?

Me   You have a problem. You can't seem to solve it. What I mean by "look to yourself" is meditating, withdrawing, getting in touch with your feelings. Take yourself away from the outside demands in order to reflect. Then, with whatever energy you have available, attempt to access the situation. Try to see what is weakening you and what is strengthening you and just try to be more *conscious.*

RDL   There are some people who are out of the reach of books, certainly. But nevertheless—here's quite a common experience. *(Laing was lighting up a cigarette and walking about the room, getting ready to swing into his story.)* A chap was telling me this in detail the other day. We all deal with this, or many of us, most of the time deal with this. He's an American attorney, a successful American attorney, forty-one years old, three years divorced from his wife, up and about and around and so on, he finds it totally useless and deeply depressing. He can't stand the depression, he doesn't want to be by himself or do nothing, so he fills all his time doing things. He's a workamaniac. That's how he turns his depression to account. He has been sinking into the morass. That way he's not very conscious. To tell him it's "in him," to go "inside," is like saying, "The way to get out of quicksand is to put yourself in it (chuckles) and you might magically come out of the other end."

Me   You're saying he's already talking to people, but he's not getting in contact.

RDL   Yes, he's got girlfriends, and serious girlfriends, and he's a successful attorney, but his life inwardly is empty. It's not that he feels what he does is particularly useless or not worthwhile.

Me   So, in other words, what good would this book do a person like that? Is that what you're posing as a question?

RDL   Well, what would any formula, whether in this book, the Koran, the Bible—he's read around—what good does it do him? What good have they (the best formulas in the world) done him? He doesn't want to feel empty. He feels that his life is an empty shell, or that it's a fleeting shadow passing by! He is right, but instead of rejoicing, he's depressed. He's keeping himself going, but his inner life has evaporated, the zest is gone. Instead he's left with fretting and worrying, should he watch the baseball game or what not.

Me   So, has he come to this realization?

RDL   Yes, that is what he's telling me.

Me   So, I don't know what good telling someone to do something is, if they don't have the powers within them to do it, but what I <u>would</u> tell him is what use he might make of the book if he was looking for that. I would say, "Right, if you say you feel empty, there's something missing. Every once in a while you must get a glimpse of what it is you're missing, otherwise how would you know it was missing? You must see it in somebody else." So first of all I would try to make him conscious of that much. Keeping a notebook of these events can help.

RDL   He's quite conscious of that sort of thing.

At this juncture I was beginning to wonder if some of Laing's characters who weren't in a position to avail themselves of "how-to" books were really partly autobiographical. They all seemed to

desire change without being willing to do something about it.
Otherwise why was Laing talking so much about those who cannot
use books to help themselves, while we were, after all, attempting
to create such a book? This was a little like discussing the design
of a photo album for the blind. I kept these conjectures to myself
and on we went:

Me   O.K. then, let's say that he (our depressed lawyer) has a few
        areas which he sees are better than others. I would say to
        him, "Well, you can leave things the way they are. Your time
        is already fully allocated to supporting what you've got
        going. There's no room for any other changes. (But if he's
        coming to you I guess he does want to make a change.) Set
        aside a certain amount of time every week and devote this
        time to this activity, to building the part that is conscious,
        that is reaching you."

        I could say specifically that I sometimes find myself in a
        situation similar to your character: overwhelmed in New
        York City with people to see and things to do, committees
        or boards, activities that eat up the time and I feel that
        nobody loves me, but I'm busy. If they want me to do
        something, and I feel that I'm in demand, I complete the
        obligations even if I feel overwhelmed, because I don't want
        to look like someone who doesn't come through. Then I pull
        out of it and watch for a while. I ask myself what pursuits
        are not empty, and when I find the appropriate ones I try to
        build on them consciously—you know?

RDL   You have to allow yourself a certain degree of flexibility so
        you can bend with it, a certain amount of fresh air so you
        can breathe in and out. You're not stuck in a fixed pose so
        that you feel you would, if you tried, melt, or move or
        de-freeze, crack.

Me   I _am_ flexible at certain times in certain areas. When I get a
        grip on myself, I move. I grow, and I move in the direction
        where I'm going to get de-frosted—I always move in that

direction. Though I sometimes get stuck, I stop and correct. People come to me for *self-marketing* advice. Everyone can avail themselves of the actual steps I tell them to take, but it requires a certain amount of courage, and usually, if they come to that, <u>usually</u>, maybe because they're paying money, they're prepared to venture forth. Similarly, if they come to therapy, they're prepared to have a look, even though they'll present some difficulties. If someone buys a "how to do something" book—"how to take care of somebody else," "how to bond" might be a better concept—then they're probably ready to move on that activity. I guess that's the best answer I can give you. To some people, it <u>would</u> be totally useless.

RDL   Yes, we were talking about this last time and although I go along with that, in a way, as soon as you present it, I find my mind immediately springs to expressing its reservations about it.

Me   Yes?

RDL   You say that whenever you're in a sort of "down" position, you "get a grip on yourself." Then you take stock of this situation and proceed in a rational manner to maximize those areas which are more enjoyable, or more heartening, or are "uppers," and you retreat as far as you can from the "downers," because you find that even if you're "down," you tend to be more up in certain circumstances and more down in other circumstances. Where you can put your chips on best, where there is a chink of light, you go for it. Fine, I've got no reservations about that at all....

Me   O.K.

RDL   Well, I <u>have</u> got reservations about that, but I needn't pick at them just now. As far as that goes, O.K.

        Now you always seem to take it that in all circumstances, the thing to do is to "bond" with someone else. There are many, many "unbonded" people in the world. Millions live lonely lives alone, or lonely lives in a crowd, at home, at work, in all those situations where there are people to exchange words with, to interplay with, to smile at, to grimace to and make eye contact with, and so forth, but there's no one in <u>our</u> sense of the word that they're bonded with. Is "bonding" the answer for all? I would think that more people are bonded than unbonded. Everyone I know personally has at least one, or two or a few relationships of love, comradeship, heart-to-heart affection, reciprocities with people they're fond of and know and trust and like and live among and so forth. The people I know are like that. Most of the people who read this book already have some bonds.

Me   I am not trying to address people who have no bonds in the world. That would be a relative rarity. When you go into therapy, you form a bond. You don't usually have no one in your life. You form yet another bond, a bond with somebody who is going to be constructive for you, you hope. *So suppose you select from your natural environment someone whom you think is going to be constructive for you, based on where you feel you want to be going, on what you particularly need. In other words you start off with someone relevant.*

RDL   Yes, but you might find—and this is one of the things that I felt this book was addressed to—you might find, looking around your personal environment, that one of the things that is getting you down is that there is no one in it, apart, among, or from those you know, or have heard of already, that you care to make an additional bond with.

Me   Would it get you down because you don't want to do that?

RDL   No. You may be reading this book in the following circumstance:

You're not going to get any more help from the environment and the people around you than you're getting already. The only person you can get more help from is yourself. The environment is the <u>status quo</u>. That's it. Your relevant environment is not going to change just because you would like it to. A magic person is not necessarily going to turn up from the last blue ridge of mountains, laced with snow, a man who knows how to make a magic bond. Maybe that he or she is just around the corner, maybe he or she is up or down the street, next door—maybe not. So under normal circumstances, you take it that the next person you meet is going to be like all the rest, whether he or she is a psychotherapist or not. So the idea under those circumstances of trying to find someone one's never heard of....

As we spoke I reflected that I did actually think that Laing was a magic person who had turned up from the last blue ridge of mountains. However impossible he sometimes seemed to me, he had a special power over me that no one else did. That, more than the speculation that he was wiser than anyone else, kept me going. Even though Laing was argumentative, he was still listening to me—responding—and trusting my intent. That intent was good, and it empowered me. Somehow his personhood was linked to my own sense of purpose in a way that gave me heart. I kept up the pace without mentioning this afterthought.

Me	Why does it have to be someone you've never heard of?
RDL	I'm taking the example of people who haven't heard of anyone wiser than they already know.
Me	O.K., right.
RDL	Just go and see a wise man. O.K. There are wise men and wise women around whom we haven't heard of. You might think the world's full of them, but I don't.
Me	Not everyone wants one.
RDL	So if you want one, go out and get one.
Me	Right.

RDL   Right. You might not trust yourself enough to be able to tell the difference between Mr. Looney or who else.

Me   (Laughing) So what do you do?

RDL   Be careful. You can certainly see that millions of people are making fools of themselves with people they take to be "wise." No one else thinks they're wise except <u>them</u> and their own followers.

(Is this what Laing partially thought of himself, I mused privately.)

Me   *I think you should pay attention to what feels good, and keep conscious of where that is.* People get depressed and they don't even know what it is that's hurting them in their environment. They're just not conscious.

RDL   Yes, but when you say to someone who is depressed, he or she can only laugh with a tortured, sardonic grimace at being told what he can tell himself or herself. One of the other tortures in depression is giving yourself all the best advice, and not being able to take it. That's one of the things which is so depressing about depression.

I found Laing's understanding of depression to be akin to an actual identification with the depressive sufferer. He had far more familiarity with this territory than with the frame of mind I was offering up to him and the reader.

Me   (Laughs) So the readers will have to get this book at the right moment—just as they're coming out of it. (Laughter) You know, the cupboards are always half empty or half full. There's always somebody who can't do anything. There's always somebody who is too immobilized to take the advice you have to offer. I think that just directing yourself to move toward the line is a constructive step. Then just keeping a record and making plans and being aware of the fact that there are going to be times when you can't make progress, and don't get punitive towards yourself, but instead just say, "why am I stuck here? How long am I going to stay this way?"

Let's say you can't take your own advice. So what would you tell people who are reasonably controlled, but feel themselves slipping? An example comes to me of a manic-depressive personality, a woman, whose doctors are pushing lithium on her, and she's afraid to take it because she knows that it has bad side effects. She doesn't really know what to do. She's scared. I have a neighbor in that state.

RDL   Well, I would give the same advice you gave. If lithium stabilizes you, but you don't want to keep on taking it, don't stop taking it right away. While you're taking it take stock of the situation. Think from your past experience, or imagine, the best situation open to you in which to be without lithium. *What facilitates you getting your balance and keeping it once you've got it? Aiming for these conditions, all the way to these conditions,* can only make it easier for you. *These conditions cannot do harm to others.*

Me   Yes, that's good.

RDL   Whatever that might be. One may be in for surprises. There's a lady who comes to see me from time to time. She's a headmistress in a secondary school, special subject English literature. From time to time she would get in a very excited state—sometimes pleasantly, sometimes not. And she almost lost her job, twice in fact. She really didn't want to lose it. She actually comes from Australia. She flies over from Australia to see me maybe twice a year or so. One of her whole things is that she's terrified to go out in the street because of fear of dogs, particularly Alsatians. And she was always in a very high-strung state.

        So next time I saw her she said she'd sat down and really thought about this—tried to clear the panic away—and suddenly the answer occurred to her and she bought herself two Alsatian dogs!

Me   (Laughing) *So the best thing to do if you're afraid may be to do what you're afraid of.*

RDL   Well, that wasn't what she felt she was doing. It never occurred to her that she wanted an Alsatian, but as soon as she did so that was that. That was the answer to that state of frantic craziness.

Me   What got her to do it, though?

RDL   Well, it never occurred to <u>me</u>. If I were smart enough, I might have done it. Anyway it occurred to her. People might go on for years in states like that without that sort of thing ever occurring to them. It sounds too good to be true, but just suddenly it sort of snaps.

Me   Did it ever happen to you like that?

RDL   No—I can't think of anything. If I think of something maybe I can bring it in later.

With the recorder off Laing confided in me, saying that he planned to separate from Jutta but had not yet acted on this plan. *Was divorce the act Laing himself was most afraid of? I wondered.*

CHAPTER NINE

Double Binds

Have you ever met anyone who claims that she would leave her present marital situation if only she had enough money? Lack of economic prowess has often kept many otherwise unsatisfactory relationships intact. The more equal economic opportunities available to women in the last hundred years have contributed to the facility with which people divorce each other.

Economic limitations have a way of restricting our freedom. Fears of potentially risky or unfamiliar situations may manifest themselves in more easily embraced economic quandaries. These economic dilemmas provide emotional stability. That's a payoff.

Often when I conducted Self Marketing workshops, I addressed this issue of the potential rewards for failure to earn the income that the participants professed to desire. In the service of this task I asked the individuals to list all the consequences of success, both negative and positive. This is an illuminating exercise. It began like this: *Do you find yourself in a double bind? Do you have to lose something or someone in order to succeed? How does success change your scenario for you?*

The professional medical community refers to the sometimes elusive benefits patients get from keeping the very symptoms they say they want to be rid of as "secondary gain."

I wondered if Laing gained any extra benefits or secondary gain from his persistent negative cash flow. His talents seemed to me to be a lot more extraordinary than his monetary needs. I was therefore looking for covert motivations. Laing had incisively pointed to the protection against overly exciting sexual encounters in my case when I carried an extra thirty-five pounds of weight.

I speculated not just about the payoff for my own self-defeating behaviors, but about what Laing's rewards might be for being locked into the chronic economic bind of spending more than he was earning. Without intending to trivialize either Laing's economic quandary or the difficulties I had in taking my own advice here, I wanted to explore the depth and texture of all complicated patterns of behavior that I was trying to change. I knew that whatever the secondary gain, reality still had to be dealt with if a permanent change of behavior was to come about.

In the ensuing discussion I tried to draw Laing out a bit in this elusive arena of double binds or "damned if you do, damned if you don't."

Me   You know what's interesting about money? I do a Self-Marketing Workshop designed to find markets for people's natural talents. I always explore people's attitudes about money in the workshop because a lot of participants say that's what they want. And yet they don't seem to do it. They seem to have all the capacities necessary, and you wonder, "What is it that's preventing them?" Is it lack of skill, lack of direction? Sometimes it's something underlying all of this. One wonders what would happen if they actually did what they said they wanted to do.

            And the consequences are sometimes so negative. For instance, suppose you are responsible for someone else, your spouse, perhaps, and you are angry with this someone else. If you earn anything extra, half of it is the spouse's. Actually, there's a punishment involved in earning, a punishment that you're not really able to discuss or bring out in the open, because it's not acceptable. After all, you're supposed to be the bread winner. It's not acceptable for your own self image, or for anything else you want to put out there. So that tends to muddy the waters as to where the disability or lack of results come from.

RDL   There's always that can of beans. I don't suppose there's any way of making a generalization about that. I think it's the Germans who called it "promotion neurosis." It's the state of affairs when someone gets depressed or goes to pieces when they are successful, when they get promoted. They can't stand being a notch or two better then they were financially, or being more powerful.

Me   It creates expectations. There's always a big hidden agenda with money, almost always.

RDL   I don't know how hidden it is always. I can think of quite a number of people who have got money or different degrees of money, and there's no particular mystery about what they want it for.

Me   Yes. The hidden agenda comes in the part which you **don't** discuss. I always find it kind of revealing when I go over my petty cash accounts annually.

(I was remembering all the money I had spent on my various quests in the past, beginning with my former professor, Bill Reynolds, and culminating in the considerable expenses I was then incurring while traveling back and forth from New York City to London and having our recorded tapes transcribed. Actually I was delighted to have earned enough money to be free to follow my interests in this way. I wondered what Laing might be thinking, just then.)

I have to go over all the things that I've spent money on. And I suppose what you're spending on is very often what's closest to your heart. You're making a choice about what to do with your money. It's always somewhat enlightening to me when I see my real direction, that is, where I put my energy, my money. In a way, you buy affection. It's not that people wouldn't love you anyway if you didn't have money. They probably would. But still, you put money in the direction of supporting that affectional system. It's an investment, so to speak.

RDL   Yes.

Me   And the way you approach it is often by the particulars of the actual process of earning, rather than by motivational aspects which might be more important. You blame the opportunities, or lack of them, rather than make a conscious choice.

So, what I always do in this workshop is have people imagine they did what they say they wanted to. The reader might find it useful to examine the probable consequences of eliminating money, or the lack of it, as a barrier, too. Look at all the different aspects of that. How would your relationships change? Suppose you were suddenly a millionaire, would there be anything you would do differently? Funny, a lot of things sometimes change. You might be confronted with freedom that you wouldn't know how to use, which is a good enough reason not to create the situation.

RDL   Again, we can never in this book really address people who are self-sabotaging, who sabotage their own lifestyle or life support system, who enter a game of pretending to themselves they want something different, but are doing other things, nevertheless, to keep things as they are.

Just as Laing was doing, I thought.

Me   Why can't you, because that changes, too? Suppose you make them look at it. (Hopefully) Self-sabotage can get pretty boring.

RDL   Oh, yes.

Me   They can fix things up so that it's not the case anymore.

RDL   Well, level with yourself and make more money that way, what you really want. Again this falls into the self-felonious type, you know, perfect vice, and nice work if you can take it. And everyone likes to think they do that, I suppose. Who does? That means there's a catch in that, I think. If you are kidding yourself well enough, then you don't know you're kidding yourself. So if you're mistaken in what you think, you're not kidding yourself, but how do you know you're not kidding yourself? You drive yourself crazy by that.

I conceived that Laing might be allowing Jutta to lose her much loved house, by not earning enough to make payments on it. Because Laing was angry that he was no longer the focus of her attention, perhaps he felt he would also erode what he had given to her? Although Laing eventually arranged to travel a great deal, visiting with others out of England for long periods of time, he never again bought a house or remarried. He had a ninth child, Benjamin, with another woman, Sue. Subsequently he spent his last years with his former secretary, Margeurita, with whom he had a son, Charles, in 1987 (his tenth child). In a hand-written will, he left everything earned after 1981 to Margeurita and Charles and the rest to his other surviving eight children and his first wife Ann. At the time of this writing, in January 1992, the will has still not been put to rest.

How do we know if we are in a double bind? As Laing brings out, how do we know if we are fooling ourselves?

We can try out a hypothesis, and see how it feels. Ask yourself, for instance (if you are habitually consuming too much alcohol), "If I stopped drinking what would happen to me?" If our support system is made up of drinking buddies, would we then become social isolates?

How much pain would we feel without the anesthesia alcohol provides? This thought has sent many of us back to our particular bottles whether they take the form of excessive malted, ice cream and cake consumption, chronic and debilitating love addictions, a costly cocaine habit, compulsive, clandestine, and heartless sexual encounters or even the rampant excessive consumerism which has put many Americans inadvertently into high-interest debt to credit card companies.

All of these diverse but *destructive behavior patterns can be used to numb the pain of life. It takes courage and extraordinary motivation to beat the odds and break the self-defeating cycles of our own design.*

CHAPTER TEN

Occupational Hazards

All of us who work are rewarded in life by the incomes and prestige we earn for the services we render to others. Just as in the classical conditioning situation of the rat in a maze who runs through complex corridors to get to the reward of the cheese, we sometimes go through our own loops to get the reward of a job well done and financial gain. The habits involved in our work become so ingrained in us that we continue, metaphorically speaking, to run down the maze long after the cheese is gone.

We have all been accosted in a social situation by someone insensitively cross-examining us, only to find that he's a trial lawyer. We have engaged in one-sided conversations and found that we have been talking to a therapist who has been paid very well for listening or a writer who is eager to share the information she has recently been researching.

The trial lawyer may carry his or her valuable cross-examination skills inappropriately to a social system, making others uncomfortable, while the therapist may bring her over-used listening skills and under-utilized conversational skills to a social situation, boring everyone to death with his or her passivity. *Every occupation has a built-in hazard. The hazard makes you less responsive to the situation at hand, less in the moment, more stylized in your responses.*

How can we adjust well to the constant flow of changing situations? *What are our particular occupational hazards?* What occupational hazard might burden Laing? I imagined that he was perhaps dwelling too long on his own painful nodes of experience because he had been so successful at writing about human suffering. Our discussion about occupational hazards follows:

Me   I was thinking yesterday about occupational hazards. You know, if you get to do something and you get paid for it, you tend to do it more than you might otherwise do it, in other situations. If you're a therapist, you're supposed to be accepting—listen to people with an open mind—and that's helpful in life as well. But sometimes, if you've been so heavily rewarded for that, you carry it into situations in which being discriminating might be more appropriate.

Or, on the other hand, you may get paid for being dis-criminating, as I sometimes do, "headhunting." Sometimes I don't enjoy people as much as I might, because I'm being too judgmental. So when you're working up a strategy to figure out where you want to go, it might be worth looking at a bent you might have, or a predisposition that's geared toward what has been financially rewarding, but doesn't have so pervasive a payoff. Does that make any sense to you?

RDL   Yes. I was just wondering. I was thinking of myself and people I know personally who are professionals, whether people, including myself, tend to fall into that. Do you really think that happens?

Me   Frequently. It's just natural. I have a friend who is a New York psychoanalyst. He stays relatively silent most of the time. You can have a conversation with him, and he'll just sit there and being an analyst, that's the role he plays; he'll just sit there in a normal conversation smiling an enigmatic smile. It works to a certain point, but it's frustrating, because sometimes I'd like a human response.

RDL   Yes. It's very sick. I mean, it's fantastic if you've got the nerve to carry it off, to really get paid very well and do little else but sit there and smile, be it enigmatically or one way or the other. And say as little as possible. The number of lines or prescriptions a doctor has to memorize in order to lay out scripts are very few. There's a few grunts and ums and ahs and hmm hmms and then maybe about twenty sentences which you can repeat for the next twenty years and get paid for that.

(I am laughing away.)

RDL   It's been one of my things that has been sort of a thread since I was a boy, a type of self-reflected skepticism. And it's very salutary, if the mind doesn't fall into an obsessive, ruminative circle. Indecisiveness and inconclusiveness are endless and completely useless. I definitely have had at different times a tendency to split into that useless type of reflectivity. And then the thing to do, I think, is simply to pull oneself out. If one can't, too bad. I think that's true for all useless internal numbers. If one decides that a number is not getting one anywhere, it's not enlightening one, it's just a waste of time, then cut it out. Why go on endlessly pursuing why one is pursuing endlessly, chasing the endless tail?

Me   Yes.

But I wondered if Laing would pull himself out of his own depressing passivity.

RDL   I don't usually get hung up on endlessly dithering in obsessional ways, but there is a choice point of when do you decide that something is a waste of time altogether? How do you know? It's not always easy to tell. I mean, I lead myself, many times, to stay in a state of mind that I don't think I would otherwise have allowed myself to stay in if I could have got over it. Because it was grist for writing.

Me   Yes?

RDL   I'm very fortunate because it really doesn't matter what state of mind I'm in, whether it's up or down, it's all grist to the mill. It's all grist to be looked at, understood, and expressed, if one can see anything in it.

Me   So that could be an occupational hazard, in a way? It isn't a total hazard. You capitalize on whatever upset you're going through, right? Observing it and writing it down.

RDL   Yes.

Me   Since you're a poet and a writer, it gets out there.

RDL   Yes. I think I would feel that's a waste of time, unless I could market what I wrote.

Me   Right.

RDL   Just keeping a private diary, I don't think that would satisfy me.

Me   You're communicating. Besides getting money, you're communicating to people.

RDL   I've got that internal expression, if I can "turn it to account." That means bringing it out and turning it into communication with the world, which will hopefully be rewarded.

Me   What's the down side of that behavior? That's the up side. It's a beautiful use of getting upset and making it constructive, getting paid for it, making it intelligible, sharing it with other people. Do you think there's a down side?

RDL   The down side?

Me   Yes. Like an occupational hazard. To me it detracts from the immediacy of the situation; you could be off sulking, hurt, anything, and you could do any number of things. One of the choice behaviors that you would have is to express what's bothering you and sort of let it go through you.

RDL   I said that one still has to let it go through one. I said everything's grist for the mill. That is true. But I also said that these countervailing considerations, for me, allowing myself to go into the sulks are enlightening; it's a waste of time. I've been in a sulk before.

Me   That's not the alternative I was referring to. That's one alternative. You sit and sulk, and that gets it over with. Another alternative is what you do to put it out constructively and communicate it to someone. Another alternative is to modify the situation, to get angry, to do something. In other words to correct for what's hurting you. It's an active stance as opposed to a more passive, reflective stance. Not that it's really passive, because you're putting out something, but you're not putting it out to where it came from. You're dissipating it.

RDL   I don't think considerations of writing affect my personal actions very much.

Me   You would do that anyway, whether you were writing or not?

RDL   Yes.

Me   I see. (not fully convinced)

RDL   I have done so. For the most part I have led a recessive life in terms of writing and reading, but I'm also in quite a lot of interchange in the family and outside the family. I don't know whether that sort of thing seems to me so ingrained, one's style.

Me   Yes.

RDL   I think I'd be dead by now one way or another if I didn't feel pretty free about being angry, when I feel angry. I don't know how some people keep it up. Never even lashing out at all, it's all pulled back.

Me   Sometimes you do other things when you're angry instead of being angry.

RDL   Yes, but I feel I can afford to, because I don't feel I can't be angry.

Me   Yes. That's an option.

RDL   There's a difference between prudent restraint under certain circumstances, and this neurotic inhibition.

Me   Yes.

RDL   It's much easier to be angry if one wants to be, or doesn't give a fuck as it were, whether one's angry or not. Not getting angry all the time is not a problem for me. I think it's ruined some people at work. It kills many people. Hatred, anger, and so forth that can't be expressed. As Troy said, the wine turns into vinegar and becomes a sort of poison, literally, in the system, and then it's like a duodenal ulcer, hypertension, or one thing or another. None of those things about keeping one's balance are ever solved any more than at the moment. I mean, it's a balancing act; you've got to keep on doing it. Even when one's got one's balance, it's always possible for the unexpected, wherever it comes from, to be a wind that one's got to continually readjust to, to keep one's balance. No one can retire in midstream or feel that the game's over and all that.

Me   You can make modifications, a change of emphasis here and there.

RDL   Yes, that's what I'm saying. It's a continued, never-ending feedback, reciprocal adjustment process. Never comes to an end or settles once and for all. So there are always adjustments being made all the time. So that's a different story from the type of situations where some people do such vital diametric change, complete restructuring of everything. Like this photographer guy. I suppose he changed occupations. He lost his job. He left his wife.

Me   Who is this guy?

RDL   The company director I told you about. He changed his focus, he changed his social status, he changed his friends, he changed his wife, he changed where he lived, he changed the food he ate, to some extent obviously, and the company he kept, and his occupation. This is a major thing to do.

Me   Yes, it's a lot of changing.

RDL   He changed his type of dress, let his hair grow.

Me   You've changed your looks in the last few years.

RDL   What, in terms of this?

Me   Yes. And your hair has grown. Isn't your hair longer than....

RDL   That's been a continued process of...that was done over time. I expect to shave all this off next week (referring to his beard and long hair).

Me   Really? (smiling.)

RDL   Yes.

Me   Why?

RDL   Because I'd like to see my face again.

From the time I first began to know Laing he had been preoccupied with the issue of betrayal. Although one must study and reflect on one's relevant area of interest to write knowledgeably about it, I thought that Laing was drowning in his depressing obsession about betrayal—and wondered whether it was, in fact, an occupational hazard for him.

I imagined that he wanted to come out a bit more and get through what I thought was a deadening anger. He drank a great deal, was often in fights, and had grown his hair long. I looked forward to seeing his face again, too, and imagined that his shorn locks would herald a lighter outlook. His handsome face was partly concealed by a trim salt-and-pepper beard and mustache which framed his sensual lips. The black and white longish hair of his head which was usually tousled fell softly around his gold-rimmed glasses and around his collar. His dark, clear, hazel eyes gave intelligence and warmth to his mobile face. Sometimes he looked as if he had seen everything, and at other times it was the opposite. His square shoulders lent shape to the roomy-gray heather sweater which he wore, and his black tailored trousers enclosed slender, wiry legs. He had well-tended, square hands which were often cradling a beer or a cigarette or playing the piano. They were strong, competent, tender hands, and I sometimes found myself staring at them for no apparent reason.

Laing leaned back in his chair, and his daughter, Natasha, then about eleven years old, came in and took a picture of him and then of me. I pieced the pictures together, but they were taken separately. He was not looking at me in my picture paste-job. Nevertheless, I adored R.D. Laing.

I looked forward to his turning his depressing obsession with betrayal to account instead of dwelling on it as an instrument of self-torture. Just before his death in 1989, he was still thinking about the injustices committed in the name of love. Issues of betrayal haunted Laing from the cradle to the grave.

CHAPTER ELEVEN

Combating Self-Defeating Metaphors

How do you fight an idea?

With another idea.

Since the dawn of consciousness we have all been subjected to other people's expectations of us, expectations which are often presented in the form of stories. We are inspired by them, motivated by them, and often controlled by them. Sometimes the original story is better suited to the purposes of our forebears than to our own. Nonetheless, we are saddled with this excess baggage as soon as we have the wits to comprehend what is expected of us. When we are young, pleasing our parents or guardians has a very high value as they are the source of our very sustenance. As we get older, if everything goes as it is supposed to in the maturational process, we look to ourselves and to significant other people to establish our own expectations of ourselves, our projected story.

However, the old story often retains a spuriously high value, regardless of whether it is good or bad for us now, regardless of whether it is at all realistic in light of our natural proclivities and abilities.

On the negative side, these inappropriate stories, from wherever they spring, are the basis of our maladaptive behavior—or neurosis, if you will. It's what the proverbial rat is driven by when it keeps running through the maze to get the cheese, even when there is no cheese there any longer. It is what people do when they live in a miserly way even though their present situation may be bountiful, because their parents lived through a depression and learned to be appropriately frugal. They may deny themselves obvious conveniences like a comfortable living space, or the joys of theater and travel, always laboring under the delusion that they are suffering through an economic depression.

Taking the system that works best for you and extrapolating to other less-functional areas can be a very salutary exercise. That is, if one is clearest and most successful in one's work—relationships—as opposed to familial relationships—perhaps trying some of the procedures used at work might increase effectiveness at home. For instance, if you easily fly into a rage at home but find that similar disappointments at work evoke an orderly, calm, scheduled confrontation, you might benefit from applying some work skills at home.

Similarly, *contradicting the inappropriate behavior or obsolete belief system of one's partner might be helpful.* During my initial meetings with R.D. Laing, I would sometimes, in my anxiousness to serve him, spring up unsolicited, to do things he wanted done, such as jumping up to find his wife for him when he expressed a desire to talk to her. Stopping me in my tracks and aborting one of these missions, he asked, "Are you going to go into every room in the house and call Jutta? Did I ask you to do that?" He made me look at my desire to serve him. This immediate feedback helped me to look critically at the all-too-common pattern of unreflectively and inappropriately serving a man, which was in accord with my upbringing. I told Laing, however, that I was happy to experience the desire to hop up and please. It was actually born of my uncommonly high regard for him. I was thrilled that Ronnie had sufficient prestige to motivate me.

Prestige has an effect that operates even when the prestigious person isn't there. When I lost Ronnie's daily attention after returning to New York, it was still his effect on me that drove me to seek out other companions who were available on an immediate basis, rather than fall into the doldrums. Then, in turn, it was their powers that began to supply me with moral support and companionship.

Without ever embarrassing me, Laing seized many opportunities to point out what he thought was inappropriate behavior on my part. He was never self-serving in this: He used his subtle, incisive insights to empower me. Once when I felt guilty about not inviting to a meeting someone who had made his spare bedroom available to me, Laing got all animated, explaining in detail his view of the proper obligations in these circumstances. His version was minimal compared to mine and did not extend to obligatory invitations. I tried to do the same for him. In private settings he was very receptive to my opinions about his behavior with others.

Laing never broke a confidence and never offered his constructive and much-appreciated observations in the presence of anyone else. Deep down, in spite of his canny maneuvers, I trusted him. Because I knew he was good, I trusted his intent.

Isolating some of these self-defeating behaviors and metaphors gradually helped me to view myself in a more favorable light. I thereby created a more enlightened internal story for myself. My emerging view of myself was eventually reflected in the eyes of a whole network of friends who came to see me in a more congenial way. I created this by acting with increasing consistency in a manner more in accord with the way in which I wished to be known. Although stating my intentions was helpful, writing them was even more useful. It was ultimately my actions that pulled out my poison arrow and allowed me to be truly loved and truly loving. With wistful steps I moved closer to a clearer reality and increased responsibility. I walked away from attractive, but poor, choices for mates, no matter what the struggle, until at last I found real requited love. This phenomenon is proverbially called *growth.*

CHAPTER TWELVE

The Price of A Lie

"The true...is the only expedient in the way of our thinking, just as the 'right' is the only expedient in the way of our behaving."

William James, 1907

To keep our social lives well oiled and running smoothly, most of us resort to deception in varying degrees. The purpose of deception is concealment. Deceptions run the gamut from polite omission through the white lie to webs of betrayal so intricate that they require constant vigilance to maintain.

The absence of deception produces a feeling of freedom. It is implicit permission to relax the censor in yourself, the editor who blindly conforms to the wishes of others in an attempt to make the world a safer place.

For much of the time I was around Laing, I felt a strong absence of deception, stronger than with any other person I had ever known.

So strong was this message to me that it was almost a sanctioning of life.

A meta-message is a message about how to understand a message. The message I got from Laing is that although deception in one's personal life may buy one a degree of freedom, it will surely cost something in terms of happiness and self-respect. **Deception is not perpetrated without a price.**

Often in life the meta-message is that the incongruent, overt behavior of one's partner may actually be a very congruent and clear—but covert or underlying—communication. If the stories one hears seem discordant or inconsistent, one might do well to examine whether the tale is being used <u>unwittingly</u> or <u>deliberately</u> to convey a concern that is close to the teller's heart but too awkward to reveal directly. When Laing seemed distressed and careworn, but talked about apparently impersonal topics, I tried to look a little closer and listen more attentively.

One evening, Jutta, Laing and I went to a poetry reading in London. There Laing had ironically read aloud the following poem that he had written several years earlier and published in 1979 in *Sonnets*. His Scottish burr was rich with dramatic emphasis.

> When I consider what you mean to me,
> It is a fact I've come to realize
> That you're my closest link to paradise
> Despite what wise men tried to make me see.
>
> They caution us against idolatry
> And tell us that we should not jeopardize
> Immortal life for anything that dies:
> And not to be bemused by mere beauty.
>
> It seems ungracious not to take delight
> In day because it turns so soon to night.
> Eternity is always here to stay:
> It's only you and I who fade away.

You are my here and now, my present tense.
I hope you will excuse my diffidence.

That book had been dedicated to Jutta, but by the night of the reading her interests clearly seemed to be running in other directions. Although Jutta had a beautiful singing voice, she sang a lovely German Schubert song, but missed a few notes when Laing accompanied her on the piano. In fact, the whole evening was off. Laing drank a great deal and was verbally assaulting everyone around. After the poetry reading Laing introduced me to a young man at the party—"She's from Brooklyn," he said. Although I hadn't lived in Brooklyn for 26 years, he was hoping to get my dander up by his outdated introduction.

Undaunted, I hung protectively about him. His pain was almost palpable and he seemed intent on spreading it about. I handed him his well-worn, leather briefcase when he left it behind. There were tears streaming down his face. "Don't come any closer," he growled menacingly. I just couldn't bring myself to leave him until he was safe, on his way home in someone's car.

The following scene took place the morning after the lamentable party. He was clearly hung over and apparently had incurred Jutta's wrath.

Because Laing was not very accessible at the time of the conversation which follows, and because we were taping it, we shared our concerns and values in the form of vignettes or stories about other people. I wanted to be sensitive to Laing without coming closer to home than he wished. This was a delicate balance to achieve.

Upon greeting Laing at our morning meeting, I said, "So, how are you?"

"Okay," Laing said. "I didn't ask you because you looked all right."

From this cryptic comment I discerned that my question was regarded as insensitive. The message he was giving me was to look for myself: He looked tired, as if he had been up all night. He was very touchy.

That morning Laing told me a story of a philandering Italian friend. The story seemed somehow disjointed to me. Therefore, to provide a sense of continuity, some of my thoughts are included here in italics as they occurred to me throughout the discussion.

As Laing revealed his friend's troubles, I had the feeling that he was really talking about an underlying disturbance of his own which he did not feel free to discuss. I was drawn to this hypothesis not only because of Laing's manner and appearance, but because his Italian character's feelings and actions didn't ring true to me. The man he described had always been a philanderer in a society in which this was completely accepted. He did not want to leave his wife and had not been discovered, but seemed sure that trouble was imminent. He feared "terrible scenes" and was suicidal. As Laing's tale unfolded on that cloudy morning, I wondered whose problems Laing might really be talking about and how the characters could be interpreted to make a more congruent story. I listened creatively as the narration unfolded:

RDL   I've got a friend in an insoluble situation. He is one of the most accomplished intellectuals, for his age, that I know. He's twenty-eight. He's Italian. He's been through one marriage to a very attractive dancer that ended about three years ago, and he's now married to a very attractive wife, and they've got a very nice baby, and he loves her, in his fashion. He's a restless spirit, always has been, doesn't see why he shouldn't be, doesn't want to be otherwise. So, most nights at 10:00 p.m., off he goes into Rome where he drinks a lot and takes his chances with anybody. He may turn up again next day, or he may not turn up for a couple of days.

He has, or had, given himself a dictum that sexuality for women and for men is a totally different ballgame. He expounded this at length to both Jutta and me on one occasion. I think it's absolute, total nonsense, but it's a very common male idea.

Me   What did he say?

RDL   He said that it had all been expounded to him by his wife. According to him, she was convinced that when women make love they are much more inclined to do it with their heart than men are. He agrees. And now he has got caught. His heart has been touched, ever so slightly, by one of the girls he came across. He has fallen in love with her. Yet, he still loves his wife. He is quite clear that if his wife should fall in love with someone else, and have the sort of affair he's having, that would be the end of the marriage, immediately, and no question about it. It would be absolutely intolerable for him. He doesn't feel he's doing her in, in any way by this affair. It is kept completely secret. A lot of complexity goes into maintaining this complete secret from his wife. "Everyone," as they say in Roma, "knows about it, except his wife." This is not at all unusual.

Me   Does she really not know, or is it that they just don't speak of it?

RDL   He's got complete <u>carte blanche</u> in principle. He's given himself that, made absolutely no pretense about it.

Me   Then she does know, I thought.

RDL   She doesn't know that he's "fallen in love," in a rather additional sense though. He doesn't think this will rock the boat. He doesn't like keeping up his web of deception. He loves both of them in different ways, at different times. He only loves one of them at a time. He's enjoying it all, he says, and he's almost suicidal at the same time.

This sounded more like torture than fun to me.

Me   He wants the whole package.

RDL   He has it.

Me   He's got it. Is that a problem then, is his wife giving him static over this?

RDL   No, no.

Me   So he has an ideal arrangement?

RDL   At the moment. But he sees already, with sad eyes, that there's no way that the whole lot of them are not going to run into a lot of pain, when the shit hits the fan.

I couldn't really imagine what Laing's character was worried about here, since he wasn't planning to make a stand.

There's a sort of problem that you're asking for. If you want that pleasure, then there's practically certainly going to be a price to pay under those circumstances, and so there's no use reading this book or any other book to find out how there is no price to pay, when there is a price to pay.

And with mobilizing the victim with this saga in mind, I responded:

Me   Yes, there's a price, but there's a bigger price to pay for doing nothing. For instance, suppose you're this man that you speak of, very creative, obviously interested in a lot of people, and new people and freedom, and you're interested in having a family which you love. He wants both, so I think he has to first of all give himself permission, or at least acknowledge what he wants. A lot of people I notice get stuck even before it reaches this stage of consciousness.

RDL   No problem. He comes from a wealthy aristocratic Italian family and is Roman, and he's just behaving like everyone else.

Me   He's just doing what's normal.

RDL   Yes.

Me   And so is his wife.

RDL   Yes.

Me   And so is his lover.

RDL   Yes.

Me	So he doesn't require any special human engineering for this?
RDL	It's all normal, and even the terrible scenes when it all comes out, these will also be normal.
Me	Yes, of course there'll be scenes. But at least he's alive and well, having a time of it—better than pushed over.
RDL	So, you're agreeing?
Me	That he's going to have scenes? I think you can minimize the scenes by a certain clarity. For instance, he happens to be born into a kind of setup that's very compatible with him except for the terrible scene. But what's the scene going to be about?
RDL	The women are compatible, you might say, with that scene, because they're the other half of that scene, but their point of view in that scene is wildly different from that of the man, hardly speaking terms.
Me	What is his wife's part to be?
RDL	His wife's never expounded her position to me, but I imagine that issues of feminine rights or fairness or anything else are for her really passed. She's a very attractive woman of about thirty-seven and he's twenty-eight and she's mainly frightened that she won't keep his interest, such as it is, for very much longer because his eyes are usually on younger women. So I think she thinks that she's just lucky to have as pleasant a time for as long as it will last. He's just the sort of character that if he did want just that, there's no arguing that he could have it. All she could do is throw an Italian rage at him, but he's quite used to that. He's completely used to that. She knows actually it's just water off a duck's back. So it would serve no purpose except to let it out of her system. Probably, he wouldn't mind. I mean, the world is full of painful, emotional moments when things turn into painful nodes.

Me   Yes, and what happens to make them worse is that people start accusing themselves of being bad.

RDL   And accusing other people.

Me   But suppose this man realizes he is always going to need freedom. And right now he's in love, so his freedom is probably exercised less than it would normally be, since he probably wants to be with the person he's in love with and have his wife and family as a secure base. Right? That's what he wants.

RDL   He's got all he expects is possible just now.

Me   Yes, but you're anticipating the problem he's going to have.

RDL   He's spinning a karmic web of destined consequence. He doesn't know what it's going to be, whether farce or tragedy, a baby, an abortion, a divorce, the reproaches of a deceived wife, he doesn't know. He does not expect to get away with it without a price to pay.

Me   Letting go of something is painful if you have an attachment to it.

RDL   He's starting to get very fond of his son.

Me   So he thinks he won't have access to his son?

RDL   Well, he'll have access to his son, but he's an Italian father. He wants his son to be at home when he's at home and to spend quite a lot of time with his son. It would be intolerable for him to think of his son growing up calling another man "daddy." No way.

Me   So he could really use some human engineering, because the system that he's provided with only allows for a whole area of very indirect communications.

RDL   Quite wrong. He couldn't be regarded as very changeable. He lives a deeply ingrained Italian and Roman style of life.

Talking to him about change is like talking about changing the architecture of Venice.

Me   Well, it's not easy to change, and maybe the system works best for him with all its pitfalls, but maybe society does change. So suppose you realize....

RDL   But he's not asking, he's not wanting to change. He'll completely spurn the very suggestion of changing anything.

Me   So he doesn't have any difficulty. He's got the system he wants.

RDL   It doesn't mean to say he hasn't got difficulties. He's not complaining about them, and he regards them as insoluble.

This sounded like familiar territory to me.

Me   So he thinks that's the way it is, there's nothing he can do? It's his life, the price you pay.

RDL   No, I don't think he feels that there's nothing he can do, but he doesn't think it's wise or appropriate to try to. And he's also interested in seeing what will happen if he does it this way.

Me   Yes, I think he's probably chosen this course for a good reason. *The course you choose is who you are.*

RDL   But many people embark on that course without choosing the way he has, and then they run into what he anticipates. He might be wrong about that, and he's not dedicated to a catastrophic, tragic end to it all. I said to him that the sooner he levels the whole thing out with Anna, his wife, the better, because it will only be much worse the longer it goes on. He's only putting it off, and if he levels right away, it's quite possible that she might accept it, as many do, and establish a friendly, open <u>modus vivendi</u>. She wasn't born yesterday, and all that is normal also to her. She probably has wondered when it would have to happen anyway.

Me   Sure, she has to know.

RDL   But he doesn't want to do it that way.

Me   Well, he thinks the repercussions will be worse, I guess.

RDL   I don't know.

Me   Well, what will she do?

RDL   At least he has walked into this situation with his eyes open. He can't complain about what has been in the cards when they come up.

Me   Well, you could take whatever attitude you choose. I mean, everybody starts with a pre-existing situation and a set of pressures, and sometimes they feel that they don't have a choice, and everything is coming at them, and the course of events is set, so to speak, but they still have a choice. They're making choices all the time. He's choosing to play a role, and the price he's paying is that he can't be as open as he likes. He probably feels partly like a heel even though it's socially accepted. I don't think he likes to lie. And he's got, obviously, a lot of capabilities. He's got a capacity to love, he's brilliant, he's got a lot of companionship, he's learning. But the part of him that he has to make a liar to keep the setup going, I think diminishes him. Now maybe that's just been my experience.

RDL   I think it does too. *I think that lying and deception can do both the deceiver and the deceived in. It always does in the deceiver.*

Me   Yes, both, equally. You absolutely lose power completely. If you can't tell the truth, and you have to keep the lie up, it's too debilitating. You can't like yourself very much.

RDL   I don't think he realizes that.

Me   Right.

RDL   He definitely doesn't.

Me   So what I think I would do first of all is to make him look at what he feels is the price he's paying, the unpleasant part, the fact that he can't share this affair which he would like to share. He probably loves his wife, but the fact that he can't share it makes him less loving to her. It makes him resent her because she's in the way.

RDL   Yes, but also, I think, he has some, and other people have, a desire for intrigue. I must say, I don't have. I've got sort of an interest in it, but it's too intimidating for me now to involve myself in it by choice. But he has definitely. He likes intrigue.

Me   Yes, that's a degree of distance too. That may be his preference.

RDL   Oh, he's very pulled back and so forth.

Me   So that's comfortable for him, that's the level he wants to play at. But now he's got something that has upset the apple cart; he's fallen in love. It's a different level of distance. Suddenly the rest may seem somewhat tarnished to him, you know?

RDL   Yes, I'm overdoing it when I say he's fallen head over heels in love.

Me   A slight infatuation.

(Both laugh)

RDL   A bit fond of her.

In life Laing felt deceived by his mother, who told him to do things for "his own good." He was suspicious of all authority. Around the time I met him, Jutta's affections had apparently wandered to other more attentive environments. As the deceptions involved in this shift of affections were revealed to Laing, he became more preoccupied with reviewing his construction and reconstruction of past events, in the light of his new revelations. His capacity for this seemed endless. He was pitched from a sea of anger and fury to the calm waves of compassion, a compassion for the plight of one who feels herself caught in a trap in which lying becomes a viable solution.

The "Normal" Lie Versus the "Abnormal" Truth

More often than not lies to conceal extramarital sexual liaisons are socially sanctioned by the friends of those adventurous souls who are out and about sexually. Even though the path to sexual adventure is made smoother by this covert web of social support, there are still consequences of the inherent deception.

Because the troublesome quest for more than one sexual partner is a common occurrence among those who find their desires running beyond the confines of connubial bliss, Laing and I examined some damaging consequences of deception and the possibility of other equally disturbing, but possibly less deceptive, paths to take:

RDL   All men cover up for everyone else. That's just never talked about. It's a totally different world. And I think all women must know it about their own lives as well. There's one Brazilian woman who interceded with me, when I was staying with them, to help her have it out with her husband. She was physically exhausted. She was singing and playing the guitar quite well, but couldn't get her voice, and he was sort of doing her in by pretending that she was no longer attractive, because he was no longer particularly attracted to her anymore. (She had had seven children and was still attractive.) But he didn't convey that this was because he was having it off elsewhere, as I was convinced he was, though he never absolutely admitted it to me.

He sort of pulled back when he saw I might not myself be entirely, unreflectively, one of the club. He would have sworn that he was faithful to her. I mean some of those guys will actually swear on their children's lives and tell a lie.

They'll pull down everything and lie all the way. No doubt that's why there's torture in Latin America. Well, if you're the spouse at the other end of that, all your emotionality, all your reading of cues, of smell and taste, of nuances of interplay, etc. are all completely subject to deliberate mis-representation; your whole world is **completely** distorted. *So if you believe him or her, because you love him or her, then you're driven mad, or you're driven really ill, driven into the grave.*

And I went on, trying by implication to shift the locus of control to Laing himself—trying futilely to jar him out of the victim mode of thinking he was expressing here.

Me   And you're lying to yourself, and you know it. (with intensity)

RDL   Well....

Me   You're getting the cues. It's just that you don't choose to read them. I mean, how could it be that a person you are living with is having a whole other life, even being in love with somebody else, and you're right near them, and you don't notice? You must be blind to them. How could you not notice something as gross as that?

RDL   Oh, you can notice it, but everything you notice is open to alternative construction.

Me   Yes, but you might want to delude yourself. I mean, could you really not notice anything?

RDL   Oh, you might want to delude yourself, but if you're under this sort of hypnotic spell, if you're under this sort of social hypnosis, or if the cues that you get are distorted, you've got to be very careful, because you might be accused of being psychotic. I'm sure that there are quite a reasonable number of people carted off to a mental hospital when they see the truth and state it, but the other side, their lie, doesn't give way, and they absolutely lie themselves into the ground.

Indeed, very few of us do not know someone who is now or has been carrying on a deceptive relationship. For many people it would be more difficult to think of someone who is an exception, someone who has not and is not carrying on a deceptive affair.

I had discovered that the capacity for intrigue tends to remain constant. In other words the tendency to deceive tends to be like body weight, always moving toward a comfortable and steady set point in most people. *It takes a strong motivation to become more honest. Empathy is fertile ground for motivation of this sort.* My own penchant for personal honesty had been jump-started years before by a strategic intervention from my father....

I can remember being a ten or eleven-year-old attending sleep-away camp for the second season; there I found myself rather unpopular with the same little girls who seemed to appreciate me wholly the summer before. I was next to last in the popularity poll and imagined that the girl beneath me, who was systematically being tortured by the others, wouldn't last the whole summer. Then what would I do? In an attempt to revive my lost popularity I took quite insidiously to lying. In a vain attempt to make myself more interesting, I told my peers that I lived on a farm with cows, horses, and chickens. Perhaps my loss of popularity had to do with the fact that I had advanced an extra grade, and the others resented me or my attitude about this upgrade, or perhaps I was more insecure, because my parents and three-year-old brother had moved from our Brooklyn apartment to a private house in the outskirts of Queens while I was languishing away at camp. Whatever my motive, my lying grew worse. It took over so that I no longer had control of it. It wasn't premeditated. It flowed.

On visiting day my parents and brother, Jay, came to visit me at the camp in the Catskill Mountains. Although I had told them repeated-

ly that I wanted to leave, they were unwilling to take me home: they had paid for the season. The sun shone brightly, but I was forlorn. Wendy Shagrin, the leader of the pack, distrustingly asked my unsuspecting father about the cows on our alleged farm. She was closing in for the kill. From the sidelines I held my breath in amazement as my father smoothly answered the suspicious Wendy, lavishing upon her details of a farm life I could not myself, have imagined. He had the good taste never to mention this incident to me, but it marked me like the burl in a knife handle. With this event my love for truth was born. Subsequently I made an inviolable oath to myself not to lie. If I slipped — and I did — I was to go back within 24 hours to the person I had lied to and tell the truth, no matter how embarrassing. Tortuously I did this until I no longer lied. As an added bonus I was rescued from camp several weeks before the season ended and spent considerable time gratefully recovering in front of the impersonal television in our new house in Floral Park.

"Those who know the truth are not equal to those who love it."
                                                    Confucius

CHAPTER THIRTEEN

The Lance of Truth

"There is a single ultimate value for mankind—never ignore right and wrong."

Abraham Maslow, Ph.D.

"Psychotherapy doesn't exist. What does exist is people interacting with each other."

Thomas Szasz, M.D.

Deception in one's intimate life can be devastating. However, there are people who seem to gain comfort and happiness from a distant and duplicitous personal life, so long as their deceptions remain convincing to those they want to deceive. Alternatively some people can no more tolerate a duplicitous environment than they can do without oxygen. I have found a surprising constancy in one's preferential set point on the truth vs. concealment scale.

If the pervasive and cumulative effects of deception distort one's perceptions and even one's whole life, the truth can provide a lance

to cut away the web of deception and its paralyzing consequences.
There are those who love the truth; there are those who come to love
it.

Telling a "truth" which has been mired in deception discharges a
tremendous amount of energy and tension. It is literally a transformation of energy. The "truth" is a stimulus for therapeutic change, if
change is what you are after. The energy necessary to maintain a
pervasive lie is consumptive, and the revealing of a countervailing truth
releases free emotional energy. This power can be used to form a more
genuine, resilient, and intimate relationship, or it can be reinvested in
establishing a new deceptive barrier to maintain the distance and
latitude one had before.

Many families and friends collude to keep a long-submerged skeleton
hidden at great expense to their aliveness and responsiveness. The
following story is Laing's example of just such a deception and the
dramatic effects of the "lance of truth":

RDL   Did I tell you about a lady who came to see me about her
         seventeen-year-old-son?

Me   I don't think so.

RDL   Well, she came to see me about her son who had been
         recommended for hospitalization for being schizophrenic
         and possibly to get electric shock to stop the process before
         it went too far. She came to see me to put this straight. Yes,
         as it turned out, it started off when the boy had been about
         fourteen; he started saying that his father wasn't his father.
         He had never got on with his father, and it had gone from
         bad to worse. After that point his father brought him in to a
         psychiatrist.

         And the thing was that his father wasn't his father, but she
         had never told her husband. (As Laing said this he ges-
         tured emphatically and looked truly animated, as if he
         were living out this drama.) The boy, of course, sensed it.

She sensed it. So what was she to do? So I said, "You've gotten yourself into this. Are you seriously going to let your son go to the wall, really go to the wall by getting him admitted to a mental hospital as being psychotic when you know he's right? Will that be more difficult to live with—to have your son ruined for life, probably, in a mental hospital, living with that thought—rather than with whatever thought you anticipate having after the eruptions that happen if you tell your husband and son? Which do you think will be worse?" She thought that was quite a clear choice, since no doubt it would be worse to live with her son in a mental hospital. So she told her husband and her son, and the whole thing evaporated. Well, I had two cases like that. Not all that many people have a sort of maddening deception that just lances, like lancing an abscess.

"If a person is to get the meaning of life he must learn to like the facts about himself—ugly as they may seem to his sentimental vanity—before he can learn the truth behind the facts. And the truth is never ugly."

Eugene O'Neill

What To Do When The Truth Emerges: Social Engineering

Seeing the truth often calls for change which involves all the perils of a trip through uncharted territory. Frightening as this may be, the possible results are quite invigorating. A thoughtful exploration sometimes reveals more varied paths to fulfilling our desires than we might previously have imagined. We become happier as our powers increase and resistance is overcome.

Although the following discussion between Laing and me remained abstract, I had a social engineering change for him in mind, since he had mentioned his intention to divorce Jutta and sell their Hampstead house. The idea of Laing as a free radical frolicked through my mind as the following discussion, which now seems more like a sermon, commenced:

Me   I think getting divorced is often like that. Before you make
          a major change you often tell yourself stories to keep
          yourself staying where you are because change is so
          frightening. You make up all kinds of things, and then they
          become deceptive. You pick the perceptions you want to
          see. You create a whole web to support what you want to
          believe and then all of a sudden, if you burst it, you drop
          all of that, and there's a feeling of relief. But if people could
          be encouraged to have a sort of checkup on themselves as
          to what they're really feeling, detach their deceptions, it
          might do them a lot of good. I mean, you can if you're paying
          attention. If you set aside the time and you are motivated,
          you can do that and get a clearer picture of where you are.

          Most people do things to keep themselves from feeling, to
          make themselves more relaxed so that they don't have to
          cope with any extra anxiety. So they drink, they smoke, they
          eat; some have a succession of sexual partners they barely
          know. Whatever it is, they just do something to escape. If
          you stop those behaviors and just watch yourself, chances
          are you'll get to notice quickly whatever you hide from. That
          takes away the defense, and then you can have a look.

          You don't have to do anything about it at first, but just have
          a look. That's the first step, to have a good look, and allow
          yourself not to have any agenda that you must see when
          you look.

          So suppose the fellow you spoke about earlier, your Italian
          friend who was having a secret affair, said he wanted access
          to his child and that he doesn't want to lie anymore. He
          wants to be with whomever he's in love with, and he wants
          to have a good relationship with his former wife, if he can.
          He wants total freedom, and he doesn't want to lie. Let's
          say he put that situation up as a possibility and looked at it,
          because he noticed that it was getting him down when he
          took a look at his life. We're making this up, of course.

He noticed that he had to make things up all the time, that he couldn't share a lot of the things he was experiencing, things that he thought were beautiful, with those around him.

So he decided to be up-front. But he didn't want to do anything foolish like jeopardizing his rights to have his son near him. I'm not talking about being impractical, but once you have practicalities kind of cared for, you might see how far you can actually go. You might open up. And maybe there's a price you pay, but there's a price you pay the other way, too. So it should be a real choice, not a default. I think that even though there's that initial period where a new set-up is very difficult, because it doesn't fit the old mold, it is worth the effort to create some kind of unique arrangement that's closer to what you want and is not guilt-ridden or full of lies.... I don't think it's wrong for someone to want to keep meeting new people or to be in love. I think that if you love someone and marry and have children, a certain kind of love develops and most often, although not in all cases, sexual excitement dies down even if you are comfortable. That's just what often happens with close proximity over a long time. It's a different thing. And most people, if they're free to, and they have that sort of energy level, look to satisfy themselves elsewhere, and if that's prohibited, they often lie. Then they close down parts of themselves, and they come to some compromise, or otherwise deny themselves altogether, and then they're angry and frustrated. So they take their anger out on their partner, and everybody gets done in that way.

If you can at least see yourself clearly, that's the first step. Then if you know what you want, it's sometimes possible to arrange for it. You'll still have a certain discord, but I think one can arrange, more or less, for built-in freedom—at least that's what I'm trying to do. I think it can be done.

RDL   I think that can be done if there are at least two people, not
        one person, two people who cooperate in doing it. There
        are also quite happy nuances of modus vivendi that exist
        successfully. There are two things here that strike me. One
        is that marriage confuses a lot of people: the sort of coupling
        and uncoupling of people, with and without children, that
        now has become usual. A so-called marriage in a registry
        office is such a totally different thing from a marriage in a
        serious, sacramental, religious rite that some people still
        adopt. The whole business of exclusive monogamy between
        couples forever comes from this marriage vow. But because
        they get married in a registry office, or start living together
        and start being regarded as a couple, or have children, they
        hypnotize themselves to go into that sort of contract though
        they never were committed to it. So there's a problem that
        this label is nonexistent, I mean, it's completely illusory for
        them. In the sort of circles that we move in you can't talk
        like that, and I think it's still very amazing to talk to a lot of
        people....

Me   Yes, but more and more people are doing it, more and more
        people just live together openly, particularly in America. I
        think more so there. I'm not sure.

RDL   Oh, everybody does it here. I don't think I've met anyone
        in the last ten years who ever thought they needed to get
        married in order to live together. I mean, getting married for
        income tax purposes is the usual reason.

Me   They make that up though. That's not their real reason. It's
        just an excuse for romance; they're just embarrassed that
        they chose to get married.

(Both laugh).

RDL   I'm not even sure whether some of my friends are married
        or not. They've been together for years with children and I
        don't even know, nor wonder, whether they are married.

During the course of these conversations, Laing stopped himself. He told me that in listening to himself speak to me he had noticed a tone of contempt or superiority in himself. He said that this was a mistake. He didn't mean it and was going to change it. It came from the feeling that I was asking him to change things that he couldn't change. But he said that he didn't want to put me off from being indefatigably positive. He said that if he did that, he might have to switch roles with me and he didn't know whether I was as good at sabotaging as he was.

Moved, relieved, and encouraged by this admission, I seized the opportunity to request that he reveal himself a bit more. Perhaps Laing had pricked himself with a lance of truth, I mused. I told him that our readers would want to hear more about him. In the back of my mind was the thought that the patient is cured when he tells you everything, a concept that is embedded in the theory of psychoanalysis. He took the cue to reveal his personal struggle in "Waking Out Of A Fool's Hell," which follows.

CHAPTER FOURTEEN

Waking Out of a Fool's Hell

"Facts do not cease to exist because they are ignored."

Aldous Huxley

"The great end of life is not knowledge, but action."

Julian Huxley

"Logical consequences are the scarecrows of fools and the beacons of wise men."

Thomas Huxley

Knowing when to act is not the same as having the strength to do so. I wondered about Laing's readiness to change his marital situation, a change which he did make within the next few years, by leaving his family in London and traveling about, eventually resettling in the Austrian Alps in a rented house. I was curious about how he had previously handled difficult transitions but had learned to control my inquisitiveness. An illustrative story emerged in the following conversation:

Me   Are you going to write down any stories about yourself for this book?

RDL   Oh, I don't know. There are those who like to make up encouraging stories for themselves: one is playing a congenial part, one has got a hopeful future, and there is a happy ending. I can never really convince myself, personally, about that sort of thing. I've never found myself doing it as a deliberate plan. I've never been attracted to directed fantasy or all that sort of framing. When I'm in a situation I don't like and don't like how I see myself, I remind myself of the illusoriness of the whole structure. I remind myself that everything that happens within the category of human interplay, in terms of all the attributions that one places on it, is all contingent on a culturally bound transitory web. It isn't real! It's easier to wake out of a nightmare than to wake out of a dream, especially a really pleasant, consoling dream. *(I wished I could awaken Laing from his own dream and get him to address himself to reality as I saw it.)*

It's easier to wake out of a fool's hell than to wake out of a fool's paradise. I'm not talking about abject poverty, famine, war, but the up and down of things in peace without desperate want.

Here is another story. I thought of it after last night. I was living with my first wife Ann and we had five children ranging from about three to nine. We couldn't stand each other, my first wife and I, at that time. I couldn't stand her at all, and I was very sorry for her, but I couldn't stand her, and that didn't make matters any better. It became obvious that the whole arrangement was for the sake of the children.

Well, I got to the point where this was really getting me down. I was in a quandary about whether to stick it out and try to make the best of a bad job, instead of having pretty well given up on trying to make the best of it, which wasn't doing any good anyway, or to leave. I got to the position that I felt it was well past whether it was my fault or her fault, and it was well past the feeling that either of us could really change ourselves.

In this quandary, I convened a council of my friends, all men. I spoke to several women about it, but all my close friends happened to be men. There were four of them; I put the situation to them, and I invited their response. Whatever it might be, I would be glad to be proffered advice, reactions, or anything. Naturally any decision I took would be my responsibility alone. I wanted to have their counsel about it though.

I didn't find this counsel particularly helpful in any obvious way, but it turned it away from a completely solitary, lonely decision, in one sense. In another sense, it had to be, anyway, my decision. Also, it gave me a chance to hear my best friends tell me I was psychotic or completely gone. One of them said that he thought I was psychotic. He was a child psychiatrist and psychoanalyst. He had a Scottish upbringing from the same department as me. He thought it was un-thinkable to leave five children. I must have gone completely psychotic. To leave was neither a sane option nor the option of any gentleman. If I was not a cad, I must be mad. This was over twenty years ago now. My wife and I parted and came back together twice, before eventually separating for good. At that time it was an enormously bigger number than now, remember.

I was interested to hear the minister presiding at Laing's funeral in Scotland on September 1, 1989, tell me that Laing told him that he was leaving the potential assets of the manuscript which he intended to be his next book entirely to his first wife, Ann Laing of Glasgow, Scotland. If this is to be believed, time and experience had evidently changed Laing's perspective. When I met the first Mrs. Laing in Glasgow at Laing's funeral, I was impressed by her elegant beauty, pride, and intelligence. Since Laing was to be buried near her home, Ann Laing said that she felt that he had come back to her at last. Apparently, during the long wait his books were not often read in her house, but their tie was never completely broken.

Human Engineering Or What's Possible?

"The mass of men lead lives of quiet desperation."
Henry David Thoreau

"Improved organization gives biological advantage. Accordingly the new type becomes a successful or dominant group."
Julian Huxley

Me   Do you disapprove of human engineering?

RDL   A lot of situations, not all situations.... Many situations are decently amenable to human engineering. They can be rearranged more than many people think they can. All sorts of little things make enormous differences. A typical situation: someone hasn't got the bonding they want in the first place; a step toward an answer to that problem may be to find human understanding and companionship, sharing and compatibility, and so forth. There is more to be found than many people believe. ***Often one's own self-image of a "down" nature, or being oneself in the sulks, prevents one from getting what one needs or wants from others.*** You can say like Fats Waller, "It's simple if you know how." The problem is with people who don't know how.

I've got no problem in walking into a pub anywhere, or into a cafe anywhere, even in places where I don't know the language; within an hour or so I may be into a very enjoyable, consoling companionability with probably complete strangers. I can do that. My life would be a lot tougher if I couldn't do that. What would I do? Do I go to the movies alone? Watch TV on my own? That's the sort of thing that is very difficult to jack oneself out of, if one's in that. And there are many people who are. Lots of people are in that all their lives and don't know anything else. They never had pals when they were in school. They were lone and lonely children. The other kids laughed at them. They had some reason to be paranoid: they were always the butt of the class. They never knew what it meant to be popular, to be in demand, to be sought after. For the bully, they were the perfect ones to be picked on. By the time they get to adult life, they are already deeply done in. It's very difficult for someone who's got no other experience than that sort of thing to convince himself or herself that life can be otherwise. You can say to them quite correctly, the past is just the past. Shape up, put on a smile, move forward, look people in the eyes, they will love you if you make them feel lovable.

Me   It's not so much just looking someone in the eyes.

RDL   Fair enough. Still, remember Dale Carnegie's *How To Win Friends And Influence People*? If you help people to like themselves more, they will probably want to have you around, especially if they do not quite know why.

What We <u>Can</u> Go For

"The art of the dreamer is to hold the image of his dreams."

Carlos Casteneda

With a spirited imagination, a modicum of courage, and a robust will most people can generate a social arrangement that may be more conducive to their happiness and creativity than the arrangement which they now have.

Many of us who are paired off in terms of living arrangements have prohibitions on our other emotional and physical relationships and prefer to keep it that way. Some compartmentalize their out-of-home relationships, never exposing outsiders to the reality of their home-based lives. This way may be the most rewarding and secure for them. Others prefer this arrangement because it is truly the direction of their desires. For those individuals this blueprint does not represent a compromise. For other people it is an incarceration, a bondage. Most of us fall somewhere in between, enjoying the warmth and security of a loving partner, while sometimes desiring a more varied and adventurous existence.

With this issue in mind I wondered:

Do I have a prohibition on other emotionally intimate relationships? On other physically intimate relationships?

In some sense I felt imprisoned; I loved Laing, who was still a married man, however unhappy. I had good friends in New York, but I was no one's main person, no one's center of the universe. I asked myself what other arrangements were possible. Could I get any closer to Laing? If I openly developed another intimate physical relationship, would that, indeed, destroy what I was hoping to move toward with Laing, or would it change it into something more in line with my desires? How much compromise would be useful and tolerable to me?

If I were to be polygamous, was I prepared to tolerate a polygamous partner?

There are those who have no idea that their spouses have an intimate sexual relationship with someone else, and some sufficiently nonpossessive people would have no objection if they or their spouse found intimacy elsewhere. Furthermore, there are some particularly bold people who actually manage to arrange open polygamy for themselves while their devoted partners remain willfully faithful. Jean Paul Sartre and Simone de Beauvior had such an arrangement.

Many scenarios are possible. The more liberated one becomes, the more variety one creates.

You may find it fascinating to wonder, what is really best for you, if you could have your dreams come true?

What is *really* best for you?

Why not write down an ideal scenario as a guidepost, and see how close you can come.

CHAPTER FIFTEEN

The Proper Dose Of Awareness

"We are like icebergs in the ocean: one eighth part consciousness and the rest submerged beneath the surface of articulate comprehension."

William Gerdhardie

"Life is not a series of gig lamps symmetrically arranged, life is a luminous halo, a semi-transparent envelope surrounding us from the beginning of consciousness to the end."

Virginia Woolf

"The historic ascent of humanity, taken as a whole, may be summarized as a succession of victories of consciousness over blind forces—in nature, in society, in man himself."

Leon Trotsky

"I regard consciousness as fundamental. I regard matter as derivative from consciousness. We cannot get behind consciousness".

Max Planck

"It is the heart that always sees before the head can see."

Thomas Carlyle

Awareness is the sine qua non of change. Although there are innumerable techniques to increase one's awareness, it is an elusive commodity, and one may *see* oneself only in a manner that is tolerable rather than overwhelming. After all, we take a long time to develop our defenses, and the prospect of casting them aside in a day is unlikely and probably inadvisable.

Writing about awareness was the ultimate challenge for me. Separated from my consciousness by the flimsiest of screens, I could feel a whole level of discourse at work, but could not write it down or think about it clearly.

The following dialogue between Laing and me took place at a time during which I was anxious for Laing to be more aware of his situation and thereby mobilize himself to change. Had I been more enlightened, I would have stopped pressing Laing to change. I was insecure about my relationship to him: Was he really my friend? My indirect attempts to elicit this sort of information from him never worked. He sometimes seemed impervious to guilt-mongering manipulations or even normal social requests for approval.

In my relentless attempt to mobilize Laing, I called forth authorities from Buddha to Castaneda to support my contentions. Laing, as usual, resisted my attempts to change him, bringing to mind the price of awareness without any love and the compassion which his name attests to (Laing means mercy according to a Scottish book of crests I had discovered in a London library).

Gradually my approach to achieving what I imagined was increased awareness mellowed. I tried to recall and re-feel what it had been like for me to become aware of something that had once persistently eluded me. Ah, yes! It meant that the elusive idea had once been too painful to think about, too awful to be considered.

I found that awareness creeps in when one is in a more relaxed state of mind, detached and full of grace. Like the swing of a pendulum awareness comes and goes: It is a flickering flame blown by the delicate emotive winds of affection. We "know" when we are more aware, more enlightened and yet this too is subjective.

Examining the many pitfalls of the illusion of increased awareness, Laing and I nonetheless came to the conclusion that for us increased awareness, whatever the price, is the chosen path to follow.

Me   Aldous Huxley said that awareness is crucial; if you can stay aware, in the present, you have a better chance of being happy. Yesterday we were talking about transference in psychoanalysis. If you get stuck in old patterns, you lose awareness. This is because the patterns may have been appropriate for you, particularly when you were a small child. Because they are not now, they cut off some of the pleasure you can create for yourself, because you are not dynamically responsive to life. So there are two or three areas I'm particularly interested in that relate to the topic of relationships.

    Aristotle wrote about friendship, on how to behave, describing different characteristics of friendship. He describes the friendship that we have talked about in writing this book which is at least partially based on utility. Let's say for one person it's just utility, and for the other, it is for pleasure or emotional needs. Aristotle doesn't think that this is a real mutual friendship, because when the utility is finished so is the friendship. It's like standard therapy. It's based on utility, but with this proposal that we are starting with, at least the utility is on both sides. And if a friendship develops out of that, fine, but you haven't lost either way because at least you still have the utility.

RDL   Yes, I suppose so.

Me   And the funny thing is that Aristotle says it's all based on proximity. You really can't just be friends out of the blue. You have to spend some time together. He says that you have to have eaten the requisite quantity of salt together before you can be friends.

RDL   Salt?

Me   Yes. It seems to be a saying of the time, I mean 400 BC. I guess people liked salt!

RDL   So, what do you think the best thing to do is? Simply free associate or mull over or discuss?

Me   I'm interested in seeing where you are at.

RDL   Go ahead.

Laing wasn't very helpful.

Me   What I had in mind is that if one of the secrets of getting more out of life is awareness, we should examine how awareness is increased. Huxley explores various different approaches. From Buddhism to Shiva there are supposed to be 105 ways to increase awareness. Castenada says that you should stalk your own behavior, which means to watch it and pick out inappropriate "doings." He says that no habit can be maintained if you change one of the "doings" in the habit, that is, one of the pieces of the habit. So if you're the kind of person who's been conditioned not to express certain feelings, then the perfect response is not to express them, because you'll be punished if you do. When you get out in the world and set up an environment for yourself, characteristically the kinds of feelings you can safely express are very circumscribed. That takes away from your spontaneity, because you always have to repress yourself. Will you stop me if I detour from what you think is true?

RDL   Oh, I prefer if you get into your own.

Me   You just want me to go on, OK?

RDL   Silence doesn't imply agreement.

Me   That's why I was asking.

RDL   I'm just listening. I'm not either agreeing or disagreeing.

It doesn't imply endorsement because I don't say anything. I don't want to have to interrupt over everything and quibble. I'd have to interrupt myself if I was doing that.

This wasn't my idea of a dialogue, but on I went....

Me   OK, so you will interrupt when it's appropriate. If one isn't getting enough out of life he may become depressed. In order to get more value from where you are, you have to update your way of behaving or change some of your habits. If you find that you are not able to express feelings, certain feelings don't get responded to. I think even more important than that is, if you are in the habit of repression, what very often happens is that you internalize that habit so you don't become conscious of a lot of your own feelings, because you're so used to switching them off. I actually grew up in a house like that where I hardly considered expressing feelings of vulnerability. It would have been totally inappropriate. There was a time when I found the expression of this sort of feeling to be indicative of sloppy thinking or weakness or just in poor taste. I found that I had difficulty communicating in a spontaneous way to a number of people.

I had a kind of exclusive relationship, almost in code form, with my father, because we could say things without using a lot of words. Not everybody else talks that way though. There have been a number of exercises that have been helpful to me in getting to the root of what I am feeling. For instance, if I want to write something, and I have difficulty sitting down and just writing, I sometimes use a mind-mapping exercise with pictures, graphs, and vectors similar to those which Tony Buzan [a British author] devised. This is particularly helpful, because I don't have to put anything down in complete form. All I have to do is get it out, whatever form it's in. I put on relaxing music, and then I write down just whatever I'm thinking of, occasionally in the form of a picture, but usually it's just words. And I have available colored pens and pencils, so that if without thinking it through fully, I find something has a kind of positive valence to me, I might do it in a color that's positive for me. I follow the flow of whatever I'm thinking with vectors. People tend to think like that, tangentially, shooting off from different points, rather than in a real logical, serial manner. Logic comes only after you've massaged it somewhat. I find that method gets things out faster for me than if I just sit and wait for the pristine form to materialize at once.

Me   Do you think that would be of any use to other people?

RDL   Yes. There's a wide spray of what is relevant for other people in anything that one's found to work for oneself. As soon as anything becomes dogmatized, that's to say, completely generalized, it loses its impact. You know, it makes me sick, this stuff about consciousness and awareness for everyone. So we've got them more aware, got them more conscious. It's a lot better for some people of the world to be more unconscious.

Me   Why is that?

RDL   Awareness and consciousness for some people bring awareness without any love and awareness without any power, and you've got to go the whole way with awareness before your degree of awareness isn't unawareness, or different forms of illusion. You have to say what awareness or consciousness is. The Nietzsche critique of consciousness in *The Will To Power* and elsewhere is still that everyone who is aware, say, of European destiny, must be driven mad. We should all give at least a bow to Nietzsche for it drove him mad.

Me   What did he say?

RDL   He said that all that happens, happens unconsciously in us.

Basically Freud is a pauperizer of Nietzsche. We only see the emergent spray of what's going on behind our consciousness. We see it with a view to dominating it, controling it, categorizing it, manipulating it, and one way or another exercising power over it. All our impetus to knowledge through awareness is motivated by power. Three things impede us: one is the essential impotence of that power, and another is the vanity of the attempt to exercise that power, and, thirdly, there's an essential misconception behind all that awareness. If someone's got a bad tennis swing, has got into a really bad habit, then the thing to do might be indeed to focus on what's wrong, to be fully aware, to externalize it, to nowadays have it photographed and computerized and played back as they do on a pattern computer analysis. There you can see the movement has got a warp in it, so you can feed that back very consciously until you get the perfect stroke. Then you build that stroke up until it becomes automatic and disappears into unconsciousness again. So the function of becoming aware in this thing is an emergency operation. Thinking is like a cavalry charge. Speaking as a thinker, you don't think all the time.

You'd drive yourself crazy if you thought all the time, were conscious all the time. I've tried to be conscious all the time, but that's a very special discipline. I wouldn't recommend it to everyone.

Me   Are you recommending unconsciousness?

I thought that Laing seemed to be creating a how-not-to book, to counteract my rampant positivism.

RDL   No, I'm not recommending anything. I'm just saying that one can see that one can try, unless the circumstances prohibit it, to be aware, like stalking yourself, sort of hunting one's self down, hunting your hidden enemy within.

Me   Hunting the maladaptive behavior.

RDL   Maladaptive behavior and so forth. Immediately a phrase of Rilke's from one of the two elegies comes into my mind. It's about the ungraciousness of kicking a habit that one loves and has become attached to, and doesn't want to leave. [2]

Me   Yes.

RDL   I mean, there's something very nice about keeping your old habits.

Me   No one is perfect.

RDL   But the way that Rilke puts it is with affectionateness, as it were.

Me   Great attachment develops.

RDL   No, of the habit to oneself.

Me   I know.

RDL   Not just one's attachment to the habit.

Me   What do you mean?

RDL   This ungraciousness of casting aside a habit that has become fond of one.

Me   How does it become fond?

RDL   Like kicking a dog out the door. That's poetry, I mean doesn't that touch you somewhere? It's difficult to translate immediately into intellectual terms, but there's an immediate sort of feeling in that line which has got another sort of wisdom about it.

---

[2] Laing is referring to the **Duino Elegies** by Rainer Maria Rilke. In the first elegy we find the phrase, "What's left? Maybe some tree on a hillside, one that you'd see everyday and the perverse loyalty of some habit that pleased us and then moved in for good."

Me   I'm not in that mode. If I were just sitting, I think I would feel more attracted to that metaphor. If I wasn't ready to act, I might like to hear that.

RDL   So it's all right?

(Actually, it wasn't all right—but working with Laing was the best I could do then, and I went on then without objections.)

Me   Yes, it's all right.

          But I mean, people don't have to get up and buy a book. They already know that their habits are sticking with them. The reason they go and buy a book is to help themselves, because they want to change.

RDL   Yes, but people's problems might not be what they think they are.

          So, they think that as long as a mode of manipulation is the answer to everything, change it. Right? There is change and change and subtle change. Maybe what someone needs to do is change the desire to change?

Me   Oh, that's a possibility—just accept where they're at and say good luck to themselves.

RDL   Well, go back to Aldous Huxley and Castenada and all that tradition again. I mean it's not as quick as that to accept where you're at. You've got to be aware of where you're at before you can <u>say</u> where you're at.

Me   If I'm going to relate to that....

RDL   All I mean by that is it's all essentially, I think, ambiguous and paradoxical. I mean it's not just sometimes. It always is, which precludes the possibility of a final statement of what everyone ought to do, to get more aware.

Me   I don't think everyone has to do it. There are people who are happy, who are content in a very limited environment. The average person comes home and watches television.

RDL   A lot.

Much of Laing's discussion left me frustrated. He often seemed to be sabotaging me, but paradoxically he selectively encouraged me to keep on coming and recording our meetings diligently, while at the same time keeping himself aloof from many others who called, seeking access to him.

CHAPTER SIXTEEN

The Acquisition Mode

"Legem non habet necessitas." (Necessity knows no law.)

St. Augustine, 354-430

"We must indeed, all hang together, or most assuredly we shall all hang separately."

Benjamin Franklin, 1776

Sometimes we experience the painful loss of people we know, love, need, and are attached to. Changes of affection, fortune, well-being, sexual patterns, health, and death itself, all bring shifts in affectional patterns, leaving us periodically with new gaps to fill. It is, of course, not necessary to abandon entirely those we know just because our original contract with them is no longer valid. A reassessment of the situation may lead one to readjust his or her expectations and make a new, more appropriate social contract, rather than cling tenaciously to the image of the person one remembers, who is of course, no longer there. The capacity to adjust to change is one measure of your capacity for life itself.

I had put my own story in perspective and viewed it through the kaleidoscopic lenses of different ideational systems. You may choose to follow the same course. If the acquisition of new people into your support system is in order, this section of the book may become particularly relevant. In it I share with Laing the technique I used to attract and engage some of the most significant people in my life, including R.D. Laing.

Plants, for example, are made up of many interrelated systems and parts. There is only one part that actually grows, the meristem or growing tip. To be in the acquisition mode, a time in which one expends a great deal of exploratory energy and self-control, requires the marshalling of all of one's resources. This is an expansion phase, part of **our** growing tip. It is advisable to go into training, as an athlete does, before taking oneself out into the jungle of other people's egos, each hungrily striving to preserve its own integrity. Unique coping strategies are worth considering in this treacherous endeavor to touch someone else's heart. There is nothing more frightening to people, after all, than other people.

Having dealt with a number of losses, I developed a rather extreme system for emergency situations that minimized the pain of loss and maximized the ability to turn it into a constructive gain. *If the energy churned up by the grief and despair of loss can be appropriately channeled through some acquisitional coping strategy, and if the mourning can be at least partially postponed until one has created a situation in which care and affection are forthcoming from a carefully chosen other, then finding a comfortable place in the world will become a reality.* I realized this when I found myself lacking a support system in time of need.

There are always particular needs for special kinds of comforting from someone who gives love. When there are lacks or gaps in these attentions, a backlog of demands or needs build up. One might refer to these as maturational needs. One may need to be hugged a lot, or to tell one's story, or to make love in seclusion for weeks at a time.

Mastering the coping strategies of the acquisition mode should lead to fulfilling some of these neglected maturational needs. These coping strategies certainly helped me, but I put a consuming amount of time and energy into my method, since my need was great.

When a quantum of comfort is achieved, one hopes that one is freed up for the next act. Although picking up new coping strategies to redirect our behavior is stressful and requires the marshalling of courage and intelligence, the results are likely to be extremely rewarding. As for me, the results have surpassed my expectations.

As one's anxiety level rises to the height of one's increased participation, it helps to keep in mind that this is not a rehearsal, but life itself. **There's no point in repeating the same act over and over again, and boring oneself to death. (The psychoanalysts call this rut repetition compulsion.)** With this in mind, observe Laing's exploration of my coping strategies for acquiring new people:

RDL   I think you're very fortunate to have the type of mind you've got, and I think it's very useful for other people to get a glimpse of that mind in operation. When you're in a tight spot, you can calculate. Few people, I think, can do that. Instead, one worries. Worry is the opposite of clear calculation. There are people who <u>can</u> calculate, but it seems never to occur to them that they can use their powers of calculation in <u>this</u> respect.

Me   Right. That's what happens; they don't use it. They could use it if they wanted to, and all we have to do is point out and show how we use it, and they'll use it. They're not taught coping strategies in school. They're often not taught it by their parents either. Hopefully, they go into therapy if they need to, and they're taught it there. Then the relationship fuels them, or maybe they'll have lucked on to a good person, as I have here.

RDL   Do you know the motto of the British Secret Service?

Me   No. Tell me.

RDL   "Never explain, never complain, and never apologize."
        (Laughter.)

Me   Well, certainly don't have regrets.

        Let's say, learn a lesson, and press on. There's no point in
        dwelling on things that are negative, except to learn from
        them. And you should learn from everything. Think of the
        process in a pleasing or fun metaphor—like being in school
        all of the time, and you won't be as likely to get stuck as you
        could if you feel that it's life and death at every point.

RDL   Yes. I don't see why one shouldn't have regrets. Maybe some
        of us have too few regrets.

Me   You can make the most of unfortunate experiences—press
        on and calculate at various points where you might be stuck,
        using your faculties to take charge of your life situation and
        to assess your resources, assess what you need, assess how
        to get it, and make a plan which is correctable over time. If
        you can't follow it, if you're immobilized, then stop and say,
        "Well why am I immobilized? What do I have to do to
        mobilize myself?" I keep talking about wanting to lose
        weight, and I've lost some weight, not as much as I want. I
        have a tendency to agonize over it. I feel like a failure, a
        disappointment, because I couldn't even do a simple thing
        that I said I was going to do. And then I think, well, let's see,
        that's not going to get me what I want, so I may as well drop
        that. So then I'm just sitting there. Well, at least I'm not
        blaming myself. I'm sitting there, and I may get very relaxed,
        sit there and look at the fire and think, "Well, why am I not
        doing what I say I want, what I'm supposed to be doing?
        Why am I not doing what I want? And then I will say to
        myself, I must still <u>need</u> something. I must need to be fed in
        a certain way.

        Now, if I'm looking for this comforting where I can't get it,
        I'm going to meet with frustration, and I'm going to be stuck
        right there.

So I have to "assess the situation."If I need more warmth and I can't get it fast enough where I'm trying, where else can I try? Where *is* it accessible? Where is there some situation I'd like? You know, that's what I switch in to. And then my whole activity, my preoccupied activity, becomes looking at the fields, so to speak, at what's out there. Whereas, normally I wouldn't be looking. I'd be concentrating on one thing.

RDL   Well, so far the results are a bad advertisement of your own method.

Me   It depends on what you mean. They're not really, because the result depends on where I was coming from originally.

RDL   You mean you'd be thirty-six pounds fatter if you hadn't used your method?

Me   Yes. Actually, I have been a lot fatter. And so far, my method has worked for me, or I wouldn't be here with you. This would have been an impossibility ten years ago. Let me explain ***my acquisition metaphor. It is actually a treatment plan based on a certain belief.*** It has worked remarkably well for me and might be useful for the reader, too. It was devised after much study of various psychotherapy and selling systems and is a system to direct the user to more loving relationships.

[I refer to the person whose interest one wants to arouse here as the "client" and think of myself as the "therapist." It is a metaphor which I assumed for the purpose of acquiring targeted friends years ago, because it gave me more staying power. It has now become integrated into my thinking. This is the basis for it.]

At this point, encouraged by Laing's unmistakable interest, I took out my then-eight-year-old, yellow notebook, filled with it's odd-sounding, but eclectic jargon, and got ready to read out my method of choice. In the interest of accuracy selections will be reproduced here, as I read them to Laing, along with his comments. However, these principles are actually demonstrated throughout our story. ***In brief they com-***

prise the skills of intimacy: telling the truth, paying complete attention, and being as responsive as you can to the person you want to attract without sacrificing sincerity.

I started off with my theoretical basis for explaining the behavior of others. These principles are not always easily comprehended by others, and true to form, Laing took special pains to get my meaning.

Me   I believe that there is an economy of needs. A client with a failure to achieve adequate intimate relationships, by his or her own definition, is suffering from a deficit of love. For maximum change, the client (the object of your attention) must be fed from as many sources as possible.

In the therapy model, as you know, we have limited resources. All human interactions, however subtle, have a positive or negative value. Any positive response is an affirmation of the client's worth (the sense of worth of the person you're pursuing). The more one is fed (through the five senses), the more energy or love is available to feed others. If the client feeds others what they want, others will desire proximity. *Intimacy is a life skill that can be learned. It is actually the skill of intimacy that we are teaching here.* I will give you 22 steps to intimacy that I worked out.

I began reading...

Twenty-two Steps to Intimacy (Lessons in Love)

1. Intimacy entails the skill to attract others, which is to satisfy their needs, and to repel them, to be able to say "yes" or "no," to repel them in order to protect one's own integrity.

2. Positive response capabilities are learned, with children, by what their friends do, and with clients, by what their therapists <u>do</u>, and not so much by what they <u>say</u>. The connection between the two behaviors should be made clearer or closer. Listen up. The patient is always communicating.

3. Because the pervasive and molar patterns of behavior we are trying to change here are long-established, the client must be fed from every conceivable source. This insures optimal change. Use all that's there to use: such as historical productions, pictures, poems. Respond to ideas, looks, moods, desires, creature comforts, food and music preferences—use every sense modality. Make the world under the therapist's auspices as responsive as possible to the client's needs. Any benefits given will be passed on. It's simple emotional economics. Is that clear, or does it sound too dogmatic?

RDL   I think you should go on.

Me   Fine. (I wondered at this point if Laing was considering the fact that these steps guided my actions with him?)

        What I used to do was accommodate. If I knew that my target person liked something, and it was not alien to me, I would supply it. I never asked for praise about it, never called attention to this, just supplied it. If I knew a person liked red, for instance, red flowers would appear. If he liked apricots, that fruit would be provided, and so on. You know, it was crazy, but it was functional.

4. So, number four is: Do what you can, without compromising yourself, to help the client with life's problems—from research to what has worked (on request), to going with them for a drive in the city, if that's what they are afraid of or what they enjoy.

5. Raise their level of aspiration. Hope is curative. All you have to do is to want what you are going after badly enough.

6. As you become more responsive to the client, they become more responsive to themselves.

7. Define goals and treatment plans together.

8. Always be up front. You're the model. There should be no disparity between the heart and the act. **Never lie.** If you do, when you can't help it, go back and tell the truth. Apologizing is a life skill. It can be learned by example.

9. Keep in mind that it is the therapist's personhood, not his or her wisdom, that is the agent of change and, hopefully growth.

10. Don't take someone on unless you really feel accepting. Positive reinforcement (love) is a very powerful thing.

11. Keep in mind that money allows you to work. Don't get hung up on money. You will automatically be paid in other ways. Everything that happens to the client happens also to the therapist. That is true, if you select people from your own natural environment (that is, based on your own emotional needs). You can't keep your gains unless you give them away.

12. Follow the thread of the client's life, be available, talk his or her language.

13. Treat the patient the way you want him or her to treat others.

Could Laing be using my method to treat me, I wondered? It certainly felt like it.

14. Structure and summarize progress and goals together periodically to give hope and direction.

15. Teach clients to know what they want and to go after it.

16. Love them to pieces. (Abraham Maslow said this.)

17. Try very hard to understand him or her. Even if you miss the boat sometimes, the client can't fail to be impressed with your efforts to understand.

18. Do whatever works. Be vigilant and open to criticism. Constantly evaluate what you are doing and what the client feels you are doing. Don't be afraid to say you don't know. Ask for help. Try anything.

19. Explain old maladaptive behavior in terms of the client's history. When things make sense, direction and motivation are easier, and the client won't think he or she is so bad. It doesn't hurt to know what's happening.

20. I think the key here is selection, because you won't get maximum pay without maximum results. And you get the best results if you can pick someone that you are able to love, who will try as hard as you do, who is smart, and who can pay in the currency you need, which may not be money. *For example, what I needed most was* understanding.

RDL   Just let me say, this is where I don't follow how you are using the word client. When you say "pick someone," are you talking about picking a client?

Me   Not a client, in the sense of one who pays money.

RDL   But then you're talking about the target person, who in your mind is the person you call the client?

(I was getting a little worried; perhaps he did not understand?)

Me   The reason for that is that I felt that I didn't have the interpersonal skills necessary to attract the kind of person I wanted, because I wasn't already doing it. I didn't have what I wanted, and I thought, what am I going to use as a metaphor to keep my behavior positive or receptive? So what I had to make up was a story for myself. I pretended to myself that I was a therapist, so that if someone I was trying to get closer to was unkind to me or tried to distance me, I did not just withdraw, which would have been my normal response.

          Instead I told myself the story that a great therapist is judged by his or her ability to tolerate the negative transference. And if the person I was after was negative to me, instead of interpreting it as an attack on me or as dislike, I would see their behavior as their way of keeping what was of value— my love—away from themselves. I would view their behavior as negative transference. So, it didn't have any effect on me. It made me immune. It was like a shield. It was a defense that worked. That's why I refer to them as clients. I really was looking for a friend, it was just my metaphor.

I didn't expect people to pay me. Money was the last thing I needed. What happens to people who go after money is that sometimes they get stuck in that model, looking for money. They often don't get past the time when they needed money. I mean, they never switch gears. So they may need friends more than money, but instead of putting the money in the service of that, they are still hunting up money. So they pile up a hoard of money which isn't worth a thing to them. They can't even spend it, and they're stuck. My idea was not to get stuck in the pursuit of money, but to change the currency into something that I really needed, which was love. Not that I mind being paid as well, at this point.

Back to the reading of the 22 points....

21. Physical affection is fine in whatever dose you can handle it. Be as physically affectionate with anybody as you want, as long as you don't do your number on them and start to clutch. If you start to clutch (make unrealistic demands) and keep doing it, the system gets blown. You'll lose your immunity, and the therapist model will go out the window.

I could see that Laing's behavior with me bore similarities to the behavior I had advised as my method of choice.

22. Get a history of all the client's meaningful relationships and look for patterns. All this attention is a form of being fed, if done sensitively.

These were the rules I used. They went very well, or I wouldn't be *here*.

RDL   How general is this technique? You pick on someone to love, and you want them to love you. The other person, in the first place, is unsuspecting.

Me   You tell them. You can tell them. Be honest.

RDL   But in the first place?

Me   Oh, in the first place.

RDL   Yes. So then you tell them. You're up front the whole operation.

I was telling Laing. In my mind he was my patient.

Me   Depending on how much the client and you are willing to accept. You may not want to walk up to someone and say, "Hello. I want you to love me." You may want to do it in doses that are appropriate. Use your judgment.

RDL   In the steps towards developing this intimacy or friendship, there is the hazard of being put down or rejected in one way or another.

Me   Right.

RDL   To guard against being demoralized or simply put off, because you don't want to be put off—you want to have the type of attitude that if at first you don't succeed, try, try again. You don't want to be put off.

            You could withdraw in good order, and not demoralize yourself. But as far as that investment in the prospect of intimate friendship with that particular person, it's gone if you give up. You don't want to give up. In order not to give up, and in order not to be demoralized, think of the other person as a client—or you might as well say a patient. But adopt the stance internally as a therapist in the ideal sense of a therapist, and in particular, learn from the way the therapist handles negative transferences. Let that go along.

Me   Depending upon what you need. If you meet with more demands than you can handle, you back off.

RDL   It depends on what you mean by positive transference. In the strict sense of positive transference, in psychoanalytic jargon, positive transference is as deceptive as negative transference, but it's more pleasant. It's more pleasant if one is in a positive delusion about oneself than in a negative one.

Me   Absolutely. There's merit to what you are saying in terms of
            the way psychoanalysts think about the transference as a
            distortion of reality. It carries over from something in the past
            that you are attaching to a person in the present. The truth
            is that some current people actually fit what you are carrying
            over from the past. You may <u>actually</u> be in love with them.
            There is always some transference when you are in love. If
            that person would like to be in love with you, and you would
            like to be in love back, enjoy yourself. That's the best there
            is.

            So I wouldn't worry about transference if a person was in
            love with me, and I was in love back. I'd say good.

*(I think I must have been smiling as I spoke, because I was thinking
that I would have said more than just "good," if Laing had been in
love with me. "Ecstasy" would have been closer to the mark.)*

            The point is that you have to regulate yourself according to
            the reality of the sought-after person's needs. So you make
            yourself accept what you see. ***If you are really good for
            somebody, they will get closer to you.*** People tend to move
            toward the light. It's just automatic. If you're good for them,
            how can they avoid you? Sooner or later you're going to
            wear them down. That's it, wear them out. It's just resis-
            tance. They don't know what to make of it sometimes, if
            they see that you love them no matter what they do. But
            they give up eventually and enjoy it. I mean, it's not so bad
            having a person who loves you and also doesn't make you
            wrong. I'm very resourceful. Most people don't mind at all.
            I haven't necessarily positioned them where I initially
            wanted them, but I haven't lost anybody who I really cared
            for either, since I started this plan. I developed an ongoing
            relationship, in some form or another, with everybody I went
            after, no matter how remote the possibilities seemed when
            I started. It works because people are hungry for com-
            munication. If you communicate with them on a level that
            they don't usually attain, they can't go away from you. It's
            like an addiction. They have to hear the truth. There's a

hunger for it. Even if it's distasteful, it's better than a lie. They'll come back.

RDL   Yes. What again strikes me is that everything you say is so much a part of your style. I suppose this can rub off on other people who would like to adopt your style. They haven't got the confidence to do so. So if they've got touched by reading about your optimism and ability to say that it works, it gives some people heart. It's easy if you know how. The people who read this are not going to have the benefit of your immediate personality.

They're getting it from the printed page. Other people might be reading this with a view of trying to emulate your success in this sort of way. I mean, we all know people whose trouble is that they can't take no for an answer, and there are other people whose trouble is that they take no for an answer. Everyone is liable to get quite a lot of "nos" from others— and if you just fold up and go away every time, then you never get very far. A lot of people who make it have as their dictum that they won't take "no" for an answer. And they persist, and they don't give up. But some don't get anywhere.

Me   The whole thing is that they must modify their approach appropriately. I'm not suggesting that people hit their heads against the wall or become obnoxious. That's not very therapeutic.

RDL   The people that I find are obnoxious are usually not aware of their obnoxiousness. That's one of the reasons they are so obnoxious. I'm always reverting to the hopeless end of the spectrum. You're perfectly right. Let's address ourselves to the people who can take advice, even their own.

Me   Those particular skills—this twenty-two step procedure—is for acquisition. Not everybody is in an acquisition mode, no matter where they're at. In other words, if you find that you don't have the proper support system, you need to go out to get it. That was a desperate measure for me. I don't think that most people need to put that much energy into it. I had to, because I felt that I wouldn't get by, and so it was necessary. I'm not out there pursuing anybody now. I'm serving where I am. (Smiling.)

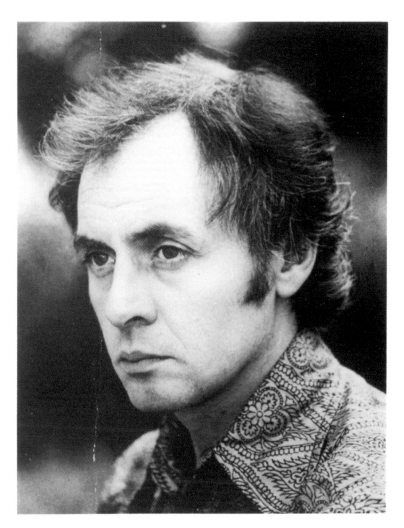

Early Portrait of R.D. Laing by John Haynes

Ann Laing, R.D. Laing's first wife and mother of five of his children, and Laing at the wedding of their son, Adrian in 1989. At Laing's memorial service which was also in 1989 Mrs. Laing said that she felt as if he had finally come home to her again. Laing is buried near her home in Glasgow at New Kilpatrick Cemetery.

Portrait of R.D. Laing by Victoria Crowe
SCOTTISH NATIONAL PORTRAIT GALLERY, Edinburgh, Scotland

Leon Redler, M.D., Laing's friend and mine, is an American psychiatrist who worked and studied with Laing since 1965 at Kingsley Hall and with the Philadelphia Association in London.

R.D. Laing at Francis Huxley's nearby London flat.

R.D. Laing in his parlor at 2 Eton Road, Hampstead.

R.D. Laing lecturing at The Open Center in New York City.
Me, rapt with attention, watching Laing at this lecture.

Contra~~indications~~ <ins>in</ins> for Reading This Book.

1. This book is about power and love. It is intended to contribute to

✓ skill^{ful} ways and means? of empowering the reader with the power to get

✓ what? ~~about~~ one wants. The power to

✓ ? get ~~wants~~ <ins>what one</ins> wants which this book may confer on you, you <u>hope</u> presumably, ~~is~~ works only if what you want, ultimately,

Laing's first draft of the "Contraindications" for this book.

Laing's empty desk at 2 Eton Road in London, one of his favorite writing places.

Roberta Russell & R. D. Laing in the New York City apartment.

One way to ~~receive the~~ benefits _from_ ~~of~~ a healing person's time ~~spent~~ _and presence_
~~with you~~ is to construct a mutually advantageous project, ~~or~~ _some_ thing to
do together which will buttress you against the ~~vicissitudes~~ _buts_ of ~~your~~ _any_
budding relationship. This "novel verité" is ~~an example of that con~~ _a' case in point'_
~~struct.~~ ~~We~~ _I_ hope that the unfolding of ~~our~~ _The_ relationship, ~~which is ac~~
~~tually~~ depicted in this book, ~~as well as~~ _together with_ the ~~subject matter~~ _content_ discussed, will help, you ~~the reader,~~ to Take Your Own Advice.

~~This book lays out~~ _What are_ the ground rules for a good relationship? ~~It~~ _This book_
gives you the chance to see the part these rules play, or do not
play, in the ~~act between the authors.~~ _relationship depicted. To me,_ ~~The~~ "technique" ~~is~~ _WAS_ largely irrelevant. Wouldn't a relationship between two (or more) ~~people who are~~ _who are_
matched on _a_ conceptual level, ~~and~~ on values, _and intent,_ ~~and~~ bound together by _mutual_
~~some mutual purpose,~~ _Intent_ prove enhancing? Assum~~ing~~ ~~that~~ people bonded by
~~this~~ utilitarian purpose, ~~act~~ _acting_ toward each other with empathy, emotional and intellectual integrity, ~~and~~ reasonably accessibl~~ity~~ to
each other, ~~this~~ should be the case? _not this_ ~~Your~~ _The_ created "game", or thing to
do together, can be much more expanded than conventional therapy and
unrestricted by licensing laws and professionalism. Courage, in the
form of transparency, ~~or the~~ willingness to come out and play, is of
the essence, and must be your guide. Laing cautions, "There is a
grave danger here, you may find a friend."

This book, _then_ is designed to show you how to increase your options, and,
thereby, _To_ be ~~better able~~ _self empowered_ to take your own advice through the enhanced

Edits by R.D.Laing of my early draft of _R.D. Laing & Me: Lessons in
Love,_ then called "How to Take Your Own Advice." Laing told me then
that he had never edited anyone's work before.

Dr. Bill Reynolds, the poetic college professor-psychologist-attorney who inspired my first application of the twenty-two steps for increasing intimacy and me, enjoying the fruits of my efforts.

Matthew Reynolds, Bill's son who is still offering rewards in the Reynolds' tradition with my husband Harold Krieger who has become my family after all and our Samoyed, Dogini.

Early snapshots of me and my mother and father.

My mother, Edith Ottenstein, with her class in New York City, 1943.

My father, Frank Ottenstein and our first dog, Sigmund, taken in 1958 .
Me at age 10 with my father and brother Jay, age 3.

Me & my brother Jay and the family house in Floral Park, N.Y.

Top: Harold Krieger and R.D. Laing in camaraderie on our last night together in New York.

Bottom: A book signing, the final evening I saw Laing. He departed wearing the red knapsack we gave him for his travels.

CHAPTER SEVENTEEN

Maximizing Possible Rejections

(How to Turn Your Loses into Gains)

"If anyone conceives that he is loved by another, and believes that
he has given no cause for such love, he will love that other in return."

Baruch Spinoza

Faced with defeat in the quest to accomplish lofty life-goals, many
people fall by the wayside, to stew in their own juices, or complain
bitterly, seeking solace in the company of other miserable creatures
like themselves. This, certainly, is a self-limiting process. Although it
can be cultivated into a way of life, the more energetic reader might
find a steady commitment to this particular tack a bit boring and most
certainly unrewarding. So, leaving the path of the chronic complainer
to our more complacent journeymen, content to hear the familiar lull
of other impotent and discontented voices, we will continue on with
exploring other avenues of action.

The authors' disavowal of chronic complaining as a less than ideal adjustment to life does not imply that a purely stoical path with no reprieve is ideal either. The secret, perhaps, is in the balance. Most of us need at least one or two fellow travelers with whom to share our travails.

I had an honest but clearly part-time arrangement in mind in my designs on Laing. These designs are brought out more specifically in this tale as it progresses—actually recorded in real dialogue as they came up between Laing and me, with the tape recorder running—a most unusual slice of life to reveal in a book. But as our tale progressed I found my desire for constancy increasing.

The following emotionally charged conversation was the last of that initial series of meetings in England. It is the unusual depiction of a real piece of life that actually happened in this novel verité. A taxi would be arriving within two hours to take me to the airport. I did not want to go.

Me   So what do you think about this project?

RDL   What do you think about it?

Me   Well, I'm in love with you, I don't know what that gets me.

Watching Ronnie's reaction, I could see there were tears in his eyes. My voice was strained with emotion, and it took a great effort to keep myself from crying.

> I've had a very interesting time. I have a little bit better judgment, probably. As far as my original proposition about co-counseling, you've gone as far as you want. I can't get slim, unless I feel enough affection coming in. I don't want to get slimmer through the effect of Tenuate, because I won't feel what I'm avoiding.

Ronnie had prescribed Tenuate for me to control hunger.

It doesn't work for me, because I won't be coming from the right source. Sometimes I feel that it's a good thing to take Tenuate, because you can get yourself where you want to be and then go out and get whatever it is you need. I don't feel that I'm at that point now.

RDL   If you base the idea of being fat or thin on whether you're getting affection, you're building a house on quicksand. Affection can go as easily as it comes.

Me   Yes I know that affection can go as easily as it can come, and I have a certain amount of affection. I'm not extremely uncomfortable in the world. I've been uncomfortable.

RDL   You want more affection.

Me   I want to have a family, some semblance of a family. Hold on. You say I'm basing it on quicksand. It's just what I need, that's all. Basing it on that, you could stop drinking this minute, and never drink again, if you felt you wanted to enough. If certain things in your life, certain stresses go away, and a balance comes, you will do less drinking and more of something else.

RDL   If you're talking to me, I don't want to stop drinking. So I haven't any problem about that. I mean, you may think I should have.

Me   Not necessarily.

RDL   At times in my life when I've been under the least stress, I've drunk even more. Sometimes.

Me   So it's irrelevant.

RDL   I don't think I regard it as a problem, but your putting on 35 pounds....

Me   It's less than that now. I've lost some.

RDL   On the scale. Unless you get more of the affections, sustained affection, family framework and children, you want to keep your 35 pounds badly enough.

Me   Closer to 26 now.

RDL   Twenty-six. You want to keep that. So if you want to keep that, then you haven't any problem. Keep it. Maybe you want to keep it, and you don't want to keep it.

Me   Actually, I just want to eat. It's hard to do one without the other.

RDL   It's just a conflict between two mortal sins, between eating and narcissism.

Me   Yes, something like that.

RDL   I find my weight is regulated by a mixture of greed and narcissism. I definitely would eat more than I do if it didn't make me fat. I don't like feeling a rubber tire around my waist. I don't know whether you regard me as fat, but...(*Laing was smiling away as he fingered his barely perceptible rubber tire.*)

Me   I wouldn't say you're fat.

RDL   But I regard myself as carrying extra stuff. I don't like the look of that. I don't like the feel of that. I feel I have noticed the difference, the feel of it, of those two kinds of feelings, desires, you might say. I mean, I don't know whether you are saying that you just desire to eat more or you would like to be able to eat more and get thinner.

Me   I don't really want to eat more. The truth is, I could do very well without eating more. It's not the eating.

RDL   You have to take your advice and penetrate as clearly as you can to what you really want. You say you want definite things.

Me	I have an idea. It's the same idea I presented to you and with you. At this point I've gone as far as I know how to.
RDL	Which is what?
Me	Well, you're finished spending time with me... (Voice cracking with emotion)
RDL	You hoped that would be therapeutic.
Me	It has been therapeutic. I feel I'm better off. And perhaps I will be better off still, I don't know yet.

Thirty percent. It hasn't been that much time So I'm reasonably optimistic. In fact, I have to certainly, at this time revise my design, and maybe permanently, and maybe for now. I still believe that if you find someone with the proper basics, and you do the things I said to you—be honest, show up, make yourself useful, and you care for the other person—you get what you want.

But, if they don't have a vacancy, and you're just upsetting their system, or you're not giving them what they need, there can be a surplus of you, in which case you had better reposition yourself or experience being a surplus, which is rejection. So now, the task is to reposition. That doesn't mean that I don't still have a bond with you. We have a lot of material; we can make a book out of it. The only way I can see it being great is if the plans that are laid out in it are exemplified with a success story, in our own persons, with whomever we do it.

We want something. We don't have it. We're in the same struggle as everybody else. We cope. Your way may be different from mine. I'm learning from you, certainly. I don't know if you've learned anything from me, but the use of our experience in this dialogue form would be great, if you come out with something that you do using your own sagacity, courage, whatever you've got to offer, and that goes for me as well.

Now if I need to have a family, I have to go out there and provide it. I thought that somewhere along the line there might be some sort of vacancy here, the way things were and because of my own desires. I'm not one hundred percent convinced that there isn't. I've just used it up for now. I think the same principles that I said work, do work. Do you disagree with them? What do you think?

RDL   What principles?

Me   *If you have a lack in your life, and you meet somebody who needs you for the things you wish to be needed for and have to offer, and they have what you want, and you make yourself useful to that person, provide some proximity and love them in a healthy manner.... If they have a vacancy, they'll move toward you. If they don't, they'll push you away.* Is that logical to you?

RDL   Yes, that's quite logical.

Me   So don't you think that's the case here, one of those things?

RDL   Yes. All of your designs on me in terms of being in love with me or hoping that you could fill a vacancy in my life that you might think is there, and so forth—I haven't got anything to reciprocate with in that respect at all. I don't know what the future holds; I don't expect that it will be any different. So I think you would be wasting your time to think that.

Me   Yes. And since you say that, and you're the best judge of that, I have to say that's probably true. So if that's the case then I say, "What do I have that's positive?" I get a lot of positives, being in love or not. I wouldn't be in love if I didn't feel the positives. If I can put out this book with you, I will consider that a great success, and furthermore, I think it will give me a lot of other options in terms of other goals. I will have more access to people who might be engaging to me.

RDL   A successful book will be a very useful success.

Me   Yes.

RDL   For both of us.

Me   Yes, both of us.

RDL   Absolutely.

Me   And furthermore, it will help me to make money in a way that's a lot more pleasing to me, and a lot closer to my interests. Which is all very well, but I think there is a much bigger game to be played, if you're getting paid for what you're doing. Otherwise you are merely a dilettante. If you walk away without at least the option of being paid, it means you're not highly regarded by the community that's consuming what you are producing.

At this point Laing sensitively gave me an opening to make the best of this crushing rejection, his lack of encouragement with respect to any romantic ideas I had about him, into a beautiful opportunity for me to excel.

RDL   What do you think makes the difference between you and the sort of man or woman, let's say a woman, who falls in love with somebody and tries to find a place in his life, and pursues him, and it doesn't work? The guy doesn't fall in love.

Me   What do I think of the person pursuing?

RDL   No, the person who gets very downhearted, very discouraged, and may even feel like committing suicide. Some people commit suicide.

Me   What do I think of that kind of thing?

RDL   No, I said, what do you think is the difference between...let me show you one of the things, if you would like, that I would tend to bring out in this book. Okay, here's your game plan, and in this respect it doesn't come off.

Me   That's not normally the case.

RDL   What's the difference between you and someone who is really shattered by that?

Me   I have several game plans. I think a lot of people always opt for the most secure path, one they know they can attain. And so they'll get there, and they don't have too many surprises.

I always walk into a situation with some gauge of the highest I can get and the lowest I'm willing to take. If I get to somewhere in between, I'll judge how I did by that. Here, with you, I had a bottom line. I certainly felt it was an honor, no matter what happened. I don't think I could have lost. That was the first half, or else I never would have come back. And I was very pleased with the first half. (*I was referring to my preliminary trip to Laing.*) I mean, I don't think that you were easy, not easy, but you're brilliant. In fact, many times you are a genius, and it's a thrill. It's a big thrill. Sometimes it's been unsettling. I've had a terrific time. It's been really exciting. I'm never bored, and this is all I'm doing. I'm not engaging in anything else. All I'm doing is just thinking about what goes on here, and anything I do is in support of that, whether in a meeting or talking to people. So the difference is that I'm going into the situation with a set of responses that are conceivable to me.

It's a very long shot to walk into a man's home which has been established for 13 years, and expect him to say, "Move over, I now need two wives," and expect that everything should mesh right in. I mean, that's really a very lofty goal when you think about it and highly unlikely.

It's not even that I'm giving it up one hundred percent, so I'm not dysfunctional. Any opportunity that came up I'd pursue. I don't intend to pursue any opportunity I don't see. I don't see any opportunity, so I'm not pursuing it. So rather than getting negative or close-minded or unrealistic about it and knocking my head against the wall, I think it's better to pursue what is positive and what is positive is this book.

RDL   The difference between you, then, and many people who are reading this book, must be that they find it difficult to operate in the world and get what they want, because when they don't get what they want, they remain attached to that and keep on trying to get it and don't see that it's impossible. They can't detach themselves.

Me   That's because they want to feel they're losing. It's comfortable. They feel bad. They've felt bad before.

RDL   So a piece of advice you'd give them then, presumably, is go for what you want.

Me   Go for broke and keep moving.

RDL   But keep moving.

Me   And cut your losses and don't look backward.

RDL   Well that implies a great deal of detachment compared to what most people are groomed to handle.

Me   Yes, I'm not totally attached to anyone or anything, which has its down side and its up side. The up side is there's nothing I can't move on, so that I feel very alive all the time. I'm never bored. It's very exciting to be alive. On the down side, I'm not bonded the way I want to be. And so the time I spend with the support system I have, I feel that is considerably wasted. It's just to keep me secure. I act as if I had the telephone attached to me on an umbilical cord.

        What I like about being here is that I've minimized that. What I don't like about being here is that I'm on the outside of everything, and that makes me look to my own resources excessively. That takes up a certain amount of energy which I would rather have put to other, more constructive uses. Does that make sense?

        I also don't like not being in control. I mean, I have no control here. I'm perfectly reactive, and that doesn't maximize what I do either, that also takes a certain amount of balancing to compensate for. So what I want now is to maximize the next task, which is getting a book out. I think we have made maximum headway on it in a relatively short time, which is excellent.

RDL   You get an offer from a publisher for an advance for a book that you promise him in June.

Me   I think that by the end of January, I can have the tapes, at least for my half, culled out and organized in a manner that I feel is saleable. However, I would have to know how much energy you have to commit and what principles you believe in. Do you know what I mean? In other words, what are you prepared to do? Let me start with this premise and see if you agree. Do you think the amount of power this book will have is directly proportional to the amount of personal growth we can accomplish and document?

RDL   I don't expect this book to be the expression of any particular growth on my part. I'm not particularly growing or developing; if anything, I'm withering away. I mean, it's not manifest personal growth on my part.

I obviously didn't believe Laing, both because I was caught up in my commitment to my own position and because the thought of Laing's withering away was too horrible for me to digest.

Me   If it becomes easier to get what you want, would you call that personal growth or increased power?

RDL   I don't know how much of anything in my life I can attribute to these meetings.

Me   I'm not saying to attribute anything to these meetings. What I am saying is that when you leave a meeting, in effect, as far as you're concerned, the meetings are completed. But how far can you go? I don't mean how far can you go with me. I mean, I have certain goals. Now you said what your contribution is at this point. You want to write a book, and you want to get the book out, within reason, and you'd like to have something you're proud of or you won't put it out, and you'd prefer a best seller to something that doesn't sell. You'd like your book to serve other people in terms of how they get what they want. To me, if they learn how to get what they want, that's <u>personal growth</u>.

I think it's difficult to teach somebody something that you don't really know yourself. I don't like to do that. First of all, it doesn't make me proud. It makes me feel shallow. And if I'm going to do something just for money, I might as well sit and make placements. It's a lot easier. So if I'm going to do something I'm proud of—where I can share what I've learned in some way that other people get it and use it and learn from it—in the process, I'll be very happy. I think that's the best thing I could possibly be doing in every respect. I think it also depends on how much movement you personally can demonstrate in the direction that you want to go. I don't mean toward me. I think you're where you want to be toward me.

RDL   But I said I didn't want to go anywhere. And that's what I'm doing. I'm not going anywhere. And I said that's fine! That's exactly what I want. I don't want to change, and so I'm not changing, and I'm glad of that. We've got this terrible metaphor of change all the time. I mean, we're all changing all the time. We don't exist anyway. We're all just flickering shadows. We come and go, etc.

Me   You can say that, but you're being facetious.

RDL   I'm not being facetious. A lot of people want to say that and haven't got the nerve to, with people trying to change them all the time. You ought to change. It would be good for you to change. You're not growing enough. You're not developing enough and if you don't realize that, we'll market another commodity, "the need to change." People who read this book also want to have the courage to be themselves whether there seems to be a change or not. That will be a change. That doesn't invalidate anything you're saying. That's just the other side of the scale.

Me   It's not the other side of the scale.

RDL   I'm a Libra.

Me   It's not the other side of the scale. You perfectly well want to change. You're a very ambitious man. You have real goals. You go after them. You'd be very disappointed if you didn't get them, and you're more ambitious than I am.

RDL   But I don't want to change in the course of them. I want to satisfy my ambitions.

Me   It's just words. You're bandying words.

RDL   And I'm doing that. (Ignoring my objections.)

Me   You're bandying words. You want this book to make money. That's a goal.

RDL   Of course.

Me   So that's a change. You don't have a best seller now.

RDL   I'm not changing me. That's not a change in me. That's a change out there.

Me   No, it's not. Out there is the way it is. What you put out is the change. What you put out is dependent on what you do, and that's what we're talking about. What can you do to get what you want? If you want a best seller, what do you have to do?

RDL   I'm an author; this is another book I'm doing. This is what I continue to do, write books.

Me   So do it!

RDL   So if there's no change in that...the fact is that it is another book and another book, that is the intention of my career as a writer and a contributor to books. And this is another book which I hope is different from every other one, and if it presumably makes a lot of money, it will enhance our reputation in the world.

Me   I don't feel my contribution will be useful until I've come closer to the mark on some of the things I need. Otherwise I feel it is not sufficiently tested. That's what's worked for me so far, but I think I have to go one step further, and I know that works on a lot of levels. So I'm sure that's true. Before I could produce something that also worked enough to be a best seller, I would have to be personally successful. I know that's true for me.

          You sometimes refer disparagingly to best sellers as a lot of junk that sells very well. Some books just don't seem to have much substance, and you and I always seem to be concerned that we don't do something like that, because it's not what we'd be proud of. I think that what makes the difference is to write from your own experience and not just picking, cookbook style, from here and there. I think there's a purpose for that, too. It's just not what I want to do.

RDL   Well, that's up to you. I mean, now you're saying that you don't think we could put this book out unless what?

Me   I'm bonded better.

RDL   Married and have a family?

Me   No, I don't want to be married and have a family. Oh God, I might never, ever get married and have a family. I would like a family though.

RDL   That's a new condition, isn't it?

Me   Never getting married?

RDL   No, no, about the book, you won't do it...

Me	I didn't say I won't do it. I said that I don't think it would be great until I get bonded. I don't mean have a family, like have a baby. I mean feel bonded to a family. That's what I think. Maybe it's not true.
RDL	Leon wanted to get married two weeks ago. (Leon is our previously mentioned psychiatrist-friend.)
Me	Oh, I didn't know that. Why?
RDL	Why? (Smiling enigmatically.)
Me	So, what do you think about that?
RDL	I'm not going to make any comments.
Me	I don't know why people get married. I got married almost by accident. I certainly wouldn't do that again. I think it's a crazy arrangement, and I'm certainly not going to have kids before I have a man around. So I'm not ready for that step. If you see something that's incorrect in the way I approach things, and you have that to tell me, I'd welcome it.
RDL	There must be men available, the kind you would like to be bonded with, who would like to be bonded with you. You say you would like to be bonded, but leaving me out of it, is that because you haven't met the right guy?
Me	You mean, is there anybody around?
RDL	There's no one that's come along that you actually want to be bonded with?
Me	No.
RDL	There are people.
Me	No there aren't, there are not.
RDL	There's no such person?
Me	No, no such person. That is, I have enough of everybody I have met. There's nobody I want more of. Otherwise, I'd

be there. I'm always right where I'm at, but what will happen is, I'll readjust and say, "Well, this is not a good place. Where else could I look?"

RDL   How can you regard that? You're out and about in the world, and in the world of business, and in other fields, being in Europe as well as America. So men are around to be bonded with. You know quite a number of people.

Me   Oh, well, I have special requirements.

RDL   Yes, whatever these requirements are which you regard as however legitimate. Are there no unfeasible requirements? Are they unrealistic?

Me   Well, they may be unrealistic. I don't know, but they are my requirements, unrealistic or not. I don't want to change them.

RDL   All right, you don't want to change them, unrealistic or not. That is to say you don't want to change them even if they're unrealistic. You might as well say you are not going to change them whether they are impossible or not.

Me   At a certain level, that's right.

RDL   That's not just a level. That's pretty basic.

Me   Well, that's my level of aspiration, but it's not attached to one person, it's attached to a category.

RDL   No, you want to find someone to bond with.

Me   Well, I want a hero. I want someone I adore, whom I have no reservations about, whom I would just want to be with, that's all. Whom I am proud of, whom I would let be free, and who would let me be free. Now that's not easy. And someone I'm learning from. I would have to be learning, and he has to be a hero.

RDL   Now how can you possibly say that whether you get that someone or not has anything to do with whether this book ought to be a success or not. I mean whether some guy like that turns up in your horizon who has a vacancy for you—and that's a major vacancy—doesn't depend on you. It depends on either chance or fortune.

Me   And me.

RDL   Well what more can a woman do?

Me   What you could do is serve in a visible way and get yourself wherever he is. That's about it. And come to his attention and be in communication. Play with him, in other words. Now, in order to play with him you have to do certain things that are relevant, which really means you have to, kind of, actualize yourself to do that. Do what you do best and do it in the best way you can. Get it out there and do it and don't sit in reserve. That maximizes the chances.

RDL   But even if so, if you do all that, it's still in the lap of fortune or fate or in the cards. It's out of your control. Therefore, it's beyond your responsibility. All you can do is make yourself available for that, but what happens is on the other side of that. Therefore you can never rest any sense of ultimate success or failure on how the external world—out there, which is transcendentally out of your control—is behaving toward you.

Me   Let me give you an example of something that counterbalances what you are quite correctly and consistently bringing out.

When a salesman sets his quota, he suggests beforehand what his quota is going to be for the month. Let's say, I'm going to make thirty thousand dollars next month. Let's say I said that, and then I did it. You could say that whole thirty thousand was subject to chance. I mean, that sort of success is all based on relationships and doing things that are intangible. But you really can't say that it is subject to the fates. It's really a question of making certain contacts and giving certain value. And it's the same principle with a relationship.

RDL   No, it's not the same at all, not the sort of relationship you're talking about.

Me   Well, how about this? If you sit in your house the chances of finding someone are very slight.

RDL   I mean, you're selling a commodity, and you know you've got that commodity and how much it's worth. You know already, from your marketing research, that it's been manufactured a number of times, and there are a lot of people who want that commodity. So all you have to do is to knock on one door after the other and depending on how good you are at backing up the commodity, some people will buy it. And if you do enough leg work, there's every good reason to believe that sales are more or less automatic.

It's a completely different ball game if you're talking about falling in love with a hero and trying to induce a hero to fall in love with you. If you think the two things have got very much in common, you'd better think again.

Me   Maybe I will. What would you suggest?

RDL   I've got nothing to suggest.

Me   You say forget about it?

RDL   Imagine what you're saying is all going to sound very funny in print. Be sure that the nature of what you call the bond you're looking for is deeply contrastable to buying and selling and money.

Me   I'm not saying there's no difference. I'm saying there are certain things you do to increase your chances of success. I don't mean that it's easy or that it's in any way guaranteed.

I mean, there are certain things that make it more likely to happen, certain behaviors that make it less likely.

For instance, if you kill yourself, your chances are nothing. That's the ultimate in inactivity. Now if you get into a frenetic state of activity, your chances are also nothing, because you're running around a totem pole. So, some kind of balance will maximize your chances for success. There's no guarantee of what's going to happen with relationships, but you certainly can increase your chances by doing certain things. Just as you can increase your chances of a best seller by assessing what it is you have to offer and who needs it and putting it in a form that is communicated to them and framing it right. Those activities will increase the chances of writing a best seller. Thinking about it and sitting in a chair doesn't do anything, if that's all you do.

RDL   Oh, no, no, I'm not disagreeing with that. But then, when you translate the love bonding thing to a sales metaphor, you don't seem to feel any dissonance.

Me   Oh, I certainly feel dissonance. I don't feel that they are the same.

RDL   But isn't that the difference between prostitution and friendship?

Me   It depends on what you're selling.

RDL   You can be friends with a prostitute. You can be a prostitute and be friends with, say, a client.

Me   If you're selling a product in business, you're calling that prostitution, right?

RDL   We're talking about emotions and oneself, and they aren't a commodity and you can't sell them.

Me   You can't buy it, but it can happen by exposure. It's difficult to happen, if there's no exposure.

RDL   Yes, but you can't buy it.

Me   Well, who's buying it?

RDL   Well, you're using the sales metaphor. What do you see then as the domain or the extent or the relevance of that?

Me   Sales is partially based on relationships. I'm not saying it is the same as bonding, I'm saying there is a similarity, that's all. I by no means equate them. It's just that there is an element of chance in sales. There are many people who could not say, "I'm going to sell x amount by the end of the month," because they don't have those variables under their control.

RDL   Well, if we go back to Levi-Strauss, who maintains that the most basic type of human relationship is exchange, it's an exchange and barter more primitive than money. I mean, you've got to get up and out and put yourself in the way of having a chance of getting what you want.

Me   The chances of a <u>knight</u> riding in on a white horse and calling at my apartment without knowing me are remote. So I'm not counting on that. So all we've got to do now is to get on with this book. To get on with the book, we should have an agreement so we know what we can expect of each other.

And on this note, I left despondently with my tapes and notes for New York to find surprisingly enough that a knight did actually come to my apartment.

CHAPTER EIGHTEEN

Someday My Knight Will Come

"The world fears a new experience more than it fears anything...because a new experience displaces so many old experiences....The world doesn't fear a new idea. But it can't pigeonhole a real new experience."

D.H. Lawrence, 1915

I left London just before Christmas, 1982. I missed the benefit of R.D. Laing's immediate presence. My trips to the refrigerator became more frequent. I wrote and rewrote, but nothing was right. Pragmatism took over. You can't write a novel verité on how to take your own advice while not taking your own advice.

The state of being in love has its advantages, but they were clearly eluding me. Cheerlessly, I continued to do the more routine aspects of writing— seeing that the tapes of our talks were properly transcribed, rewriting and rewriting again. I was not satisfied.

However, a few weeks of occasional contact with several appropriate companions fostered a good result. We set eating goals and discussed the tribulations of our accomplishments. One *business colleague, Ed, whom I hadn't seen in several years, was particularly inspiring. Having lost eighty pounds in less than a year, Ed told amusing stories of his self-supplied liquid protein business lunches consumed with associates who were eating expense account meals in elegant restaurants. He claimed that he was able to use his freedom from eating to pay better attention to the conversation and thereby do more business. Telling these stories aided his weight loss, and it certainly motivated me. Within a few months almost all of my excess thirty-five pounds were gone.*

With the benefit of a trimmer figure and a serious exercise program (one mile of swimming per day), I felt a renewed sense of pleasure in life and enjoyed the companionship and affection of my friends. Although I still harbored romantic fantasies of Laing, they were more whimsical than real. After all, he had told me very directly that he had nothing to encourage me with as far as reciprocating my feelings of being in love with him went. There was no mystery to this. I had known him, at this point, for over two years. We had spent a great deal of time together, and our relationship was still entirely platonic. I had no reason to be expecting a romantic relationship with Laing, since my desire for him had apparently not been enough to create anything more than a very trusting platonic friendship. I had even discussed my feelings for Ronnie with Jutta, who didn't seem to mind. It would be hard to imagine a safer "attachment." But of course, we had the book, which was taking shape along with me.

After a year of only telephone contact with me, Laing was coming to New York City for the first time in five years for a humanistic psychology conference held at the Vista Hotel. I had not sent any part of the working manuscript to him in the preceding year.

Thrilled that he was coming, I fixed up a room for him at my penthouse apartment. We were to spend time together for a week working on the book. When he saw me I planned to surprise him with my thirty-five-pound weight loss. He had never seen me this way. At our meeting I would be thirty-five pounds lighter and have a manuscript of which I was proud. We would be alone together in my apartment. I could not help fantasizing about him. During the course of the year he had been knighted in Sweden. Does this sound like a fairy tale? It really happened. I was awed by my good fortune and completely turned on.

So in January of 1983 a knight, Sir Ronald, did come to me. He dismounted from the commercial jet which had brought him to me from London, thirty minutes late, carrying his handleless suitcase on top of his head for balance. A large black stain of ink which had leaked from his pen was emblazoned on his white shirt directly over his heart, testifying to the ambient pressures of high flight. Overheated and overanxious, I happily claimed him as he entered the reception area, and off we went in the chauffeured limousine I had commemoratively rented for this milestone occasion. Decked out in my only recently fitting purple jeans and matching cashmere turtleneck sweater, with my mink coat self-consciously thrown over the back seat of the car, I wondered whether he was as nervous as I was. Because Laing seemed impervious to normal social demands for palliative small talk, I took everything he said to be highly significant. The air we breathed was charged. My "I'm happy to see you," countered with his halting "I'm happy to see you, too," seemed enormously important to me. The nearness of him was intoxicating. He made no mention of my thirty-five pound weight loss, but I felt that he noticed.

For conversation he opened with a report of his recent meeting with Mother Theresa: Apparently she didn't believe in abortion (which didn't surprise me), and he didn't either. I agreed almost too eagerly; I didn't think abortion was something one came away from unscathed; it would not have been for me. I did think it should be legal, though. Just in case I hadn't caught his drift, he also asked apologetically whether I had had any venereal diseases. I said "no" and asked him right back. His reply was also a smiling "no."

Upon our arrival I presented him with his own room, beautifully appointed, but the year before when I had offered him use of the empty second-bedroom at Francis's Hampstead flat, he had said that he didn't do that kind of thing. Nevertheless, I had cautiously removed the clothing I would need from my bedroom in order to avoid a potentially embarrassing situation. He took me in his arms

*and kissed me. This time he had something to encourage me with.
Of course, I cannot really describe the luxury of this experience,
but it changed me forever.*

*We celebrated my birthday together. I felt reborn. We lived together
for a week and were rarely apart. He played my Steinway with
haunting beauty, his exquisite sensibilities reverberating through
the sounding board of the old wooden piano. We told each other
stories and at times wrote well into the night. Sometimes I would
sit at his feet, and he would edit my writing. He said he had never
done this with anyone before. He wrote the following poem and
left it around the house for me:*

> The age demanded
> that we sing
> and cut away our tongue
>
> The age demanded
> that we flow
> and hammered in the bung
>
> The age demanded
> that we dance
> and jammed us
> all in iron pants
>
> and in the end
> the age was handed
> the sot that it demanded.

He was fully immersed in the beauty of his own sadness and anger.

*Once when we were in my apartment, just being together without
any particular agenda, tears ran down his cheeks. He made no
attempt to change his state, but just let the feelings pass through
him. He asked me if I knew why he was sad. It felt to me as if we
were one person. I had never before experienced the complete
lack of any barrier between myself and another human being. He
let me be. Once, in an intimate moment, he asked me not to let*

him go. I laughed and told him that there was no chance of that. Somehow, he was in my unconscious. I never got him out. I don't want to, either. Two weeks before he died I told him this. I told him that he was part of my sense of purpose. He just listened, but I think he liked it.

When we went out to New York restaurants, Laing often asked me to take the lead in both restaurant and meal selections. He seemed very interested in knowing the fabric of my existence, the way I lived, where I walked, what I ate. He looked attentively through my copious stock of books which lined the walls, once selecting a little-known William James volume that seemed to amuse him because it extolled the virtues of saying "no" as opposed to "yes." I had all of Laing's books proudly displayed on an eye-level shelf of the ceiling-height bookcase, but he never mentioned this. He said my apartment was very subtle, infusing me instantly with pride. With very few words he always made me feel that he noticed everything.

Later that week we were stretched out on a soft gray flokati rug before the fireplace. We watched the fire dance, smelled the sweet fragrance of hardwood burning, and drank wine. I was never happier. I loved him completely. I savored these moments. I tried to explain how incredible our closeness was to me, but he stopped me, saying it was the same for him. He said we would always do something together. He said he loved me, too. I was entranced.

He had been right. I was able to have my choice of men at 35 pounds lighter. And so after all my balancing and adjusting and rationalizing, it was transference revisited. In January, 1984, I made the following entry in my diary (after two separate New York City visits from Laing):

Transference Revisited

He has returned to me. Linked to my heart, immutably. Once more I am free to play in the world; to see, to feel, to touch, to smell; to strut about and then to be humbled, to search, to find, to lose myself again. But nonetheless, inextricably bound I am for the timeless moment.

Discharged early in the game, direct from my mother's womb into a sterile, empty, plastic box, I awaited him. I can hear his heartbeat now and feel the heat of him around me. I taste and feel the salty wetness of his tears upon my skin. His smell lingers on the towels I hesitate to wash long after he has flown away. Always, he will return to me, the sign of the dove.

First, as my father came to me, majestic and comforting, he touched me with his eyes as if I was god to him. Of course, I have always loved him. He's what makes my heart beat fast and my eyes dance. He lifts me up. I walk very tall.

You see, he thinks I'm good. He doesn't have reservations. He trusts me. He's not afraid. He needs me to love him. So I love him.

The funny thing is, that no matter what he does, I have this feeling that I've always loved him. It's an ache, a passion, a longing. I just love him.

He's been through me like a shaft of light.

Is that what god is?

This intimacy was real, but it had to last a long time. After that extraordinary week I was left with the heavy burden of making sense of this incredible, encapsulated experience.

Late one afternoon during our initial time in New York together, again warmed by the fire, we were listening to the beating of the rain on the surrounding terrace enclosing us. There was a big bowl of fruit and a fresh loaf of crusty bread and cheese on the round alabaster table. Apparently still training me for something, he had told me always to have bread in the house. We had fasted together the day before at Ronnie's suggestion and had broken the fast only that morning. Since he had told me he liked a soft-boiled egg in the morning, I had bought a special cup for him. His favorite brand of cigarettes, which he had difficulty getting even in Hampstead, were in a silver box on the coffee table. I never asked for his acknowledgement of these attentions. This only made his appreciation keener. The peace of that moment pervaded my soul.

Ronnie seemed comfortable. He wore a thick brown terry cloth robe I had bought at Bloomingdales for this occasion and sat at the piano which he had been playing. I was at the other end of the room just listening and feeling blessed. Then he casually mentioned that he liked having a fireplace, a piano, a garden, and children around him. I could not help but notice that we were in the presence of everything but the children. And so, taking what was an extremely long shot and a deep breath, I asked, "Would you like to have a baby with me?" I thought he would probably say "no," but I asked anyway because it seemed so right to me just then. He didn't say "no." He said, instead, that he would consider this possibility. One of his considerations would be how Jutta would feel about it. He wanted to consider it, not talk about it.

My heart quickened.

Laing's consideration of having a baby with me gave a new reality to my fantasy life. After all, he was not the sort of man who would consider a step of this magnitude lightly. He had completely discouraged me the year before. I knew he was not just being polite! He chivalrously explained that he was honored by my desire to have a baby with him. He had already sired eight children, five with his first wife and three with his second, and he even had a grandchild. That was a consideration as well.

Nonetheless, I was ecstatic. I envisioned sharing in some of the Laings' family life, with Jutta and their children in London, with me living here in New York with our child. I thought that we could get together about once a month in New York or London or wherever our interests took us. This was an unusual idea, but I didn't see why it wouldn't work.

Although Jutta was by this time openly leading the life of an independent woman — her lover had become a friend of the family — I took pains to avoid any duplicity about the situation which had evolved between Laing and myself. I called Jutta in London the next morning and asked her what she thought about the idea of my having a baby with Ronnie. She said crisply, "That's between you and Ronnie." Although Jutta was not an advocate of this plan, my communications to her remained clear and open. Laing told me she had a bit more to say to him about this prospective arrangement when he came home. He evidently got a rise out of her: our London friends told me that she hit the roof. But whatever passed between Laing and me, Jutta and me, or Laing and Jutta about this matter, it was not fraught with duplicity. I looked for signs of Laing's having denied his consideration of having a baby with me to Jutta, but although I spoke to her frequently, none emerged. She knew I was waiting for his answer. This was an unusual idea, but I didn't see why it couldn't work. The Laings already had an unusually independent arrangement.

Laing actively considered the attractions and distractions of this proposed arrangement for five months. During that time he was only intermittently available for telephone conversations with me.

In June of that year, I arranged for him to receive publicity while he saw, for the first time, the play, "Mary Barnes." The main character was based on Laing himself, and although it had originally been performed in London, Laing had never seen it. He came again to New York. I financed his trip as an advance against any potential revenues he might gain from his half of our book royalties. In spite of my longing for him, I was painfully aware of his motivations. No publicity, no trip. Soon after his arrival Laing ended my persistent speculations about our potential life together as would-be parents of our own child. Haltingly he presented me with his long-considered decision. He told me that he did not want to have a baby with me. He said that he did not want to have another baby with anyone at this time in his life. He had thought about it. It did not feel right to him. I was in despair. I felt that I would never love anyone else with whom I would want to have a child. Laing's absolute rejection of my now well-embellished dream of having a baby and a permanent lifelong attachment with him stunned me.

We had a psychedelic experience reminiscent of the sixties. He said he had never seen anyone harmed by this sort of release. I thought that relaxing reality would help me.

The edges of the high-roofed room became softer. Laing sat impassively on the tan leather Bastiano sofa facing the piano, as I backed away from him, the horror and finality of his words reverberating like an echo through a hollow cave. I found myself wandering out through the open glass doors to be alone on the terrace, a 60-foot expanse wrapping around the apartment. With consciousness stretched, I leaned far over the edge. There would be no surviving that jump, I thought. Looking back tentatively, expecting to see Laing appearing protectively behind me, I saw only the potted pines swaying and the blue morning-glories climbing mindlessly up the brick chimney and through their black nylon trellises, moving unfailingly toward the light. No response from Laing. I drifted away from my 17-story overhang, feeling the futility of life without him as my connection. Memories of old disappointments spooked me while thoughts of my concomitant creative adjustments asserted themselves in counterpoint. I moved slowly without focusing clearly, thinking that Laing must be very confident in my strength and will to live; surely he knew how disappointed I was. I credited him with great prescience and love. I was moved by his faith in me.

I returned to the living room. Laing, the repository for all my projections, was still on the couch, no inquiries forthcoming. I sat down next to him, crying sorrowfully. He didn't run away. He said he was sorry. I felt very real, surprisingly natural, and unashamed. All my senses were heightened by the trip and my exhilarating awareness of death and life. My experience of intense emotion in Laing's presence without the familiarity of the old numbers, of guilt and blame, put me in virgin territory. He didn't turn off, but he wasn't manipulated or manipulating either. I felt his sorrow too, not guilt, just sorrow.

He was good to me and gave me a safer place than I had ever known before to vent the strong emotions I was feeling. Years earlier, in the presence of my therapist, I had not been willing or able to produce the expected tears.

Laing wasn't afraid of me or for me. He comforted me. But most of all he let me be. I was never stifled, and no matter how difficult it was for him, he stayed with me. He held my hand. And when I emerged from this despair, I felt safer, more fluid, less angry, and more balanced.

In the calmer hours that followed, I felt weak and cleansed, the way one does after surviving a prolonged high fever. I was intact, but looser, and slipped naturally into analyzing what had happened between us, my best defense. I was searching for the object lesson.

Barefoot and smiling, Laing, in good-humored self-defense, said he wouldn't discuss his reasons for having considered this baby-with-me scenario for five months until he had his shoes on and was outside. I wondered why. Later that afternoon we went for a walk along the East River, entering the walking path at 60th Street and continuing until the eighties, where we reversed the process. Characteristically, he was tracing my normal habitat like a stalker, and I felt embraced.

Finally, he admitted that we had colluded to perpetuate the notion that he might want to have a baby with me. (However, when we discussed this pivotal issue again, years later, he danced around it, without acknowledging his contribution, shoes notwithstanding.) Even then, on the riverside path, it was a sensitive point for him, and he actually refused to discuss his reasons for considering having a baby with me. Refusal was always his inalienable right. Laing didn't feel a question necessarily required an answer. Perhaps he thought that an honest answer from him might redirect my interests too quickly? He was, after all, a reputed expert on the mystification of experience.

Many months after our shod confrontation I came across a book by Clancy Sigal, **Zone of the Interior,** *which I was told was a fiction that was really about Laing and his "sanctuary" in the sixties. Sigal had evidently been there, living in Kingsley Hall, the therapeutic community. I wondered why neither Laing nor his cohorts had mentioned this book to me. I hungrily devoured Sigal's account of Dr. Willie Last, a famous Scottish psychiatrist who took LSD with his patients and founded a therapeutic community. Tragedies of Dr. Last's rejected patients were described in plaintive detail. When Last lost interest in one particular young woman as a patient, she told him she would kill herself if he would not give her an appointment. He didn't. She did.*

I called a psychiatrist-friend who had worked with Laing in the community from its beginning. I asked him if things like this had really happened there. Yes, he said, they had, but he prudently added that he had been in the hospital recovering from pneumonia at the time.

When I called Clancy Sigal who was now teaching journalism in a California university, he was reluctant to talk to me. He said he didn't know who I was. Why should he trust me? I felt I had entered into some strange battlefield. Did I know that Laing had had, **Zone of the Interior** *recalled and banned? he asked. I hadn't known it. Now I did. My perspective was becoming broader. Laing's report on Sigal, although not especially revealing, provided an alternative construction for Sigal's vitriolic account, but nonetheless Sigal, through his book, helped me to gain perspective and strength.*

But before Clancy Sigal's sobering revelations, and in the calmer hours when Laing and I were able to discuss how our situation had come to pass, we decided that it had actually turned into a "setup." From my side of the tale, this setup was not unfamiliar. In fact, it bore a striking resemblance to the presenting complaint I conveyed to Laing during our first meeting in London in 1981. Then I had described my old pattern of falling in love with men who were married or otherwise unavailable to me. I tried to look back over the events of the previous five months objectively to see where I might have exercised better judgment. I always do this when I'm disappointed, to see if I might turn a painful experience into a learning experience. Perhaps I might have been more realistic?

With the benefit of hindsight, I could see many cues that I had chosen to ignore. For instance, if Laing had been seriously considering having a baby with me, why didn't he want to talk about it more? Why hadn't he called me often and initiated getting together? Sometimes the most obvious answers are the hardest to see. This, I imagine, is the veil of distortion that we wear before our eyes when we are "hopelessly in love." Although the heights I experienced were ecstasy, I did not wish to remain deluded. Disillusioning myself without anesthetizing myself as well would take more than logic. It would take forgiveness, before my knight would come again.

Most important to me was the fact that Ronnie Laing, regardless of his other covert motives, had both literally and figuratively brought me home again. On our next meeting, in London, he put me up at their beautiful Victorian house in Hampstead, in his study. Although this was not what I had planned, he had stood up for me to Jutta and brought me back to sleep in his house. I was not stoned, ousted, or rejected as long as Laing was my protector. This was a good place and setting to allow the process of healing to do its work. Having worked through my destructive and persistent tendency to recreate primal expulsion scenes, I was about to venture forth unencumbered, on a road not taken, a path in the real world that combined ideals with action.

The Kierkegaardian Knight of Faith

Transference reframed and positioned outside the therapist's office, in its natural habitat, may also be called being in love. By any name, this phenomenon is a powerful motivator: It is the cause of some of humanity's greatest accomplishments and conquests. Kierkegaard, the nineteenth-century Danish philosopher, introduced the concept of the "knight of faith"—one who is distinguished by his willingness to will one thing. This singlemindedness provides a natural armor against the ambiguities of life, lifting one above all worldly misfortune, just as falling in love often does. It is a consummate faith in one's purpose that defies ostensibly contradicting evidence.

One evening while I was in my apartment devouring Kierkegaard's work, Laing phoned up from Iona, an island in Scotland which he often used as a retreat. I had gotten into the habit of reading every author Laing mentioned, and he had thereby introduced me to Kierkegaard, whom he held in esteem. Alone in New York City, I was deliriously happy, because I had been introduced into the world of knights of faith. According to Kierkegaard, both men and women are eligible for knighthood if they can transport themselves into this realm of consciousness. I loved Laing completely, beyond all reason, beyond reality—nothing he could have done would have made me stop. And when he called I told him so—I told him that he was my knight of faith. He sighed contentedly on hearing this confession, and I knew he was moved.

A knight of faith is empowered by his or her faith to do great things, to withstand misfortune without complaint and to take great risks. I had made my living as a headhunter—putting computer professionals together with their employers. I wondered what would happen if I extended my head-hunting to putting world leaders together, specifically if I introduced the world-famous R.D. Laing to Donald Klein, a powerful psychiatrist who was a leader in the very same psychiatric establishment which Laing had defied.

Klein was regarded as a veritable potentate in the psychiatric fellowship; on the surface his procedures seemed diametrically opposed to Laing's. Klein had found that it was generally more sensible to try carefully prescribed drugs with disturbed patients, and he went on to use talk therapy only if drugs were not effective. Laing often spoke out against the misuse of drugs to control disturbing patients. At the other end of the spectrum from Klein, Laing feared that drugging involuntary patients would deprive them of the possible therapeutic outcome of their uninterrupted journey into madness. What would happen if I not only introduced Klein and Laing, but facilitated their relationship so that they grew to understand and love each other? Maybe I was in a position to arrange such a match?

I had introduced myself to Donald Klein by inviting him to be on a cable TV talk show to discuss my book, *Report on Effective Psychotherapy: Legislative Testimony*, several years before. The talk show hostess, Mary Mangin, had asked me to find a debating partner from the psychiatric establishment, and I couldn't think of anyone more prestigious. Donald Klein and Paul Wender had jointly written a book, *Mind, Mood and Medicine*, in 1981, the same year that I had published my book. Klein was a professor of psychiatry at Columbia University, Director of Psychiatric Research at the New York State Psychiatric Institute, president of the American College of Neuro-psychopharmacology, and past president of the Psychiatric Research Society.

He was a very smart hombre, and I was honored to debate with him. He was gracious, as well, in explaining—as requested—an esoteric statistical procedure before our debate. Essentially he agreed with the findings I presented in the *Report*, adding only that physiologically caused problems should initially be treated pharmacologically. He thought that psychiatrists would make better use of their time if they limited themselves to educating, diagnosing, and prescribing drugs and left the talk therapy to other non-medically trained therapists. After the debate he gave me a copy of his book and signed it "For Roberta Russell, friend and colleague." And he acted accordingly, inviting me to professional parties and to his home to meet his family and he shared the benefits of acquaintance with his influential peers and even arranged for me to stay at Queens College at Cambridge University in England when I mentioned that I wished to go there.

A knight of faith is really a warrior, a warrior so brave that he can put down his weapons and take off his armor. In this spirit, I told Laing of my intention to introduce him to Klein. He was receptive, and by way of a non-defensive introduction, Laing offered to allow me to show Klein his then-unpublished autobiography. It was therefore with high hopes that I invited Klein to read Laing's still-formative autobiography. Klein, who thought Laing was a poet, and definitely antiestablishment, read the manuscript in short order. That was in 1984. He responded with the following letter to me and did not speak to me again for five years:

Office of Mental Health
New York State Psychiatric Institute
722 West 168 Street
New York, New York   10052

August 24, 1984

Ms.Roberta Russell
R.R. Latin Associates, Inc.
404 East 55th Street
New York, N.Y. 10022

Dear Roberta:

Thank you for sending me the manuscript by Laing. I must say that I find it annoying. It is full of simple mis-statements. For instance, when he says that psychiatry is the only branch of medicine that treats people against their will, he hasn't spent much time on a Geriatric ward or in Intensive Care Units. These patients are regularly disoriented, confused, delirious, etc. and they are regularly medicated despite this condition, and without their consent. That might not be entirely admirable on the ethical level, but it is usual pragmatic medicine, and not peculiar to psychiatry at all.

Psychiatry does not imprison patients. That's a state process that does depend upon psychiatric input, but for that matter, input from lawyers, relatives, etc.

The issue here is that he quickly equates deviance with illness. Once you accept that equation, then medical practice does indeed look like social control. I am taking the liberty of enclosing an article of mine that discusses this.

I agree with him that Kierkegaard is not necessarily schizoid. He may just be a poor creator of prose, but that Laing finds him clear as crystal I find quite astonishing. It is that probably more than any single statement in this book that will bring his grasp of lucidity into disrepute.

To play psychoanalyst it is obvious from Laing's description of his parents that he transferentially identifies them with psychiatrists who he perceives as being assaultive to people for their own good. He is very clearly suspicious of anyone who tells you that it is for your own good. I sympathize with that. It doesn't mean that anyone who says that is necessarily incorrect.

Cordially,

Donald F. Klein, M.D.
Director, Psychiatric Research

In 1989, I asked Klein for permission to quote his letter in my book, and I questioned him about the intervening years. He said that he didn't realize I had tried to reach him and he resumed his supportive attitude. I was bewildered by my disappointing failure to connect these two extraordinary men. Klein's grandfather had been a poet, and there was poetry in Klein, too, I thought. I reasoned that all poets spoke the same language—the truth—and that Klein and Laing were more alike than they at first appeared. Poetry has a life of its own, outliving the poet. So perhaps this placement is still pending....

CHAPTER NINETEEN

The Art of Forgiveness

"Forgiveness is an experience of suffering in time; it may require very great suffering and for a very long time. In fact all that...man may cherish most clearly of his images may need to go forever. And this giving may happen in advance, before any reason can be found for it, in faith, and in the absence of any success or reward."

"Life needs courage above all other virtues; but perhaps the greatest example of all human courage is forgiveness."

E. Graham Howe

Forgiveness has a healing quality. Perhaps this is because the energy required to stay angry at someone is an energy that turns off part of your aliveness. It is rigid, relentless and controlling. It detracts from the angry person's flexibility and range.

Of course, anger must follow its progression and is necessary to protect us from the aggressions and improprieties of our fellow human beings. So when the swing of the pendulum leads you to forgiveness—don't fight it. But remember that just because you have forgiven someone who has hurt you, you do not now have to spend your life with him or her. We must keep our lives up to date if we are to remain vital.

The capacity for forgiveness cannot necessarily be summoned at will, but one can create an atmosphere, a predisposition for it. Having done so, provocative occasions are more likely to evoke a forgiving manner, rather than continuous, robot-like, angry behavior born of purulent resentments.

Just because you forgive the significant people in your past for any injustices they may have inflicted upon you—real or imagined—doesn't mean that you must now also throw away your good judgment, along with your anger. The lover who abandoned you, the friend who betrayed you, may do so again. Everyone has limits to their growth. The ability to see people for what they are allows us to come to terms with our experiences instead of seeing life through a diaphanous veil of romantic illusion.

Nevertheless, acting in a loving way with the people we love, even if they are rather broken down at the moment, is a lot more self-empowering than keeping oneself sealed away in splendid isolation. The balance between your heart and your mind is the key. *Forgiveness opens the heart to healing grace. It is a capacity that increases with practice, just as your muscles get stronger with exercise.*

Sometimes the quickest route to our goals is circuitous. Wisdom and love and knowledge will all take you to the same place—at home in the world.

When we suffer from life's disappointments and hurts, viewed through our perceptions of the loss of those we love, it often becomes necessary to close off in self-defense. In a sense we go into a state of shock and withdraw from the field of battle so that we may tend to our own survival and not be destroyed. Our reserve support systems take over and part of our essence or aliveness is cut down. But after the shock is over, the natural healing process begins. Bit by bit, it is possible to come to life again. Hardships that don't destroy us will only make us stronger. In our own time, as we heal, we may open our hearts to truer love, not hazed over with illusions and wishful thinking. Those parts of ourselves which we have frozen in order to provide a natural anesthetic to the pain of loss—those tender memories and shared interests can be reclaimed and we will now be able to see reality in a clearer, warmer light. Stronger and finer, we may go on enriched, if this is the path we choose. But this path requires the courage to feel again the renewed pain from which we at first recoiled—to feel again the presence of another person. And alone, to relive, in safer quarters the once intolerable drama that shocked us into a less painful numbness.

As the tentative feelings and acts of forgiveness emerge—so will we, fuller, richer, more equipped for life and more forgiving to ourselves as well. The hard rigid edges of anger melt into a soft, yielding responsiveness to life renewed. Forgiveness is a regenerative process.

If we remain angry over a long period of time, we tend to recreate scenarios reminiscent of the original traumatizing event that sealed us off in the first place. Freud referred to this as **repetition compulsion.** While stalking our own behavior, a clear pattern, reminiscent of these more primal dramas often emerges. A degree of detachment and objectivity available to us only after the healing process is well under way must be there before we can successfully undertake this arduous task.

I was sufficiently invested in Laing so that his attention provided a safe audience, heralding the release which is born of truly being myself in the presence of a caring and sensitive person. This helped to lance the boil of deadening and self-limiting encapsulated hostilities, angry feelings to which I had given no name. The psychic cancer of anger unreleased can cripple and kill our spirit, forcing us into lifeless and repetitive behavior, whereas emotional release allows us to move on to the next act in the drama of our lives. I was fortunate to have created the opportunity that followed....

On June 6, 1983, just before leaving New York City to return to London, Laing played a beautiful rendition of "The Man I Love" on the piano. "Some day he'll come along, the man I love...," the words say and off we went. The following conversation was taped as we were driven to the airport:

RDL   You've repeatedly brought up that we ought to address ourselves in what we are writing to the issue of forgiveness.

Me   Yes.

RDL   Though however important that issue is, I don't see how you see forgiveness weaving into the dramatic structure of the story we're supposed to be writing.

Me   I'll tell you how without having in mind how far I want to go with it. I'll just tell you how it's been appropriate for me, this forgiveness idea, this weekend.

RDL   <u>This weekend</u>.

Me   Beneficial, yes, and perhaps before, but this weekend, perhaps we can look at that more clearly. When I get stuck short of where I say I want to go, which is this business of having a baby and all that I want. If I'm thinking about what I'm doing and going at it with an open heart, there's no reason why I shouldn't get what I want as long as I can see what I'm doing clearly and get reasonable feedback.

So there must be something that I don't do, that I don't see, because I haven't been able to make that connection. So I figure that the error of my ways, so to speak....

RDL   What do you mean there's no reason why you shouldn't get what you want? There's every reason why you shouldn't get what you want.

Me   I don't think so. I don't see why. If a person wants to have a baby with someone, why can't they do that, unless they're doing something wrong? I better have a look at what I'm doing and change somewhat. Now, I think the power to change doesn't just come from looking at the situation. I think that whatever makes me <u>want</u> to keep that distance is whatever anger I have towards probably my father or maybe other men that followed him where I've carried out the same number.

In other words, I can't trust anybody that much. To have a baby with a man, I really have to trust and admire him.

RDL   Well, that's obviously to do with the past.

Me   Yes.

RDL   Presumably it goes back to your father.

Me   Yes, presumably, and from what I can remember, it does. I mean, it makes sense that it does. I live alone. I'm not so heavily involved with anyone except you who I feel safe enough to really cry with or do anything with any kind of real emotional release. There's almost nobody and when I do get emotional, it has been short-lived and not very gratifying. So I don't make a habit of that. It's very rare. I don't have any opportunity to ventilate certain feelings or to get them out.

It's not only that—the normal times people express themselves that way are when people close to them die. You usually commiserate with those around who are left and somehow you sort of get on with things. But every time somebody has died who was close to me, a whole block of other people associated with that person also left completely. My friend Richard, with his entire family. My father and his entire family. My mother and her entire family. Until I was cut off from almost every single person that I knew from the past. So our experience together this weekend has helped me.

"The basic formula of all sin is frustrated or neglected love."

Frans Werfel, 1944

No Accolades for Falling in Love

Me	I'm afraid to be the right weight, in the right place at the right time. I may be afraid of someone who is actually available to love me <u>and</u> have a child with me.
RDL	It's not a lot safer, it's a lot more dangerous to live with someone that way. Are you familiar with the *I Ching*, trigram 61? Did I bring it out before?
Me	No, you didn't bring it out.
RDL	It says at one point that it is asking for enormous trouble and in the long run it has to be unsagacious to become dependent on an inner accord with the one one loves.
Me	I know. But there's a stage where you have to do that. That's all. You can't skip to no attachment. You have to first suffer through the whole business if that's what forgiving....
RDL	Well, you've lived all these years and survived after 8 years of marriage, on your own and surely that proves that however painful that is.
Me	It's a lot less painful than being married has been.
RDL	It's the safest option you have.
Me	It <u>is</u> the safest option I have.
RDL	You can call yourself your own boss.
Me	Yes, and I intend to keep on doing so.
RDL	Falling in love and living with someone you fall in love with is literally the most dangerous thing one can do.
Me	I know it is.
RDL	And it doesn't get a special accolade from me, because falling in love is not the same as love <u>at all</u>.

Me   What do you mean?

RDL   I mean, you can love someone you fall in love with.

Me   Yes.

RDL   But you can hate someone you fall in love with.

Me   Yes.

RDL   I've known people who hate the person they fall in love with.

Me   But it's so energizing when you fall in love.

RDL   Oh, <u>good</u> for you.

Me   It <u>is</u> good for you. It sure is good for me, let me tell you. I like getting up in the morning when I'm in love. Very nice.

RDL   Fine, yes. So if you then give up your independence and get married or start living with somebody, sharing and intertwining your economics and the place you live and all the rest of it as well as being in love and having a sexual relationship, then what you are saying is that....I've seen what a terrible thing happens when out of two people in love with each other, one of them falls out of love while the other of them stays in love....

Me   Yes.

RDL   That's often a catastrophic disaster. It could be smoothed out, but often it leads to murder and all sorts of things.

            It's either terribly painful, terribly depressing....So you're practically certainly going to run into that.

Me   Yes.

RDL   So as the *I Ching* says, it takes you to the heights of heaven or to the depths of hell, seeking or becoming dependent upon an inner accord.

Me   But you can't skip that phase. You have to go through it. I mean maybe some people are born right there.

RDL   Oh, I'm not saying you can skip it.

Me   So long as you're not skipping it, and you have to go through it, stalling isn't going to make it happen faster. It's going to make it happen slower. So if you go for the opportunity to go through it, you'll go through it.

RDL   Yes. Yes. Oh, you don't have to tell me that. I've been through the mill of love.

Me   **Have you**? (laughing)

RDL   Oh God, yes. (both laughing)

Me   Well, how's it been for you, the mill of love?

RDL   Oh, I've got no complaints.

Me   (Laughing)

RDL   In the court of love, the accuser is always wrong.

Me   I've heard that. (laughing)

   (He had told me this before.)

(Both laughing)

RDL   If you presume to be a lover, you can't make any accusations.

Me   That's right.

RDL   And that means forgiveness doesn't arise, because all is forgiven in the first place. It's carte blanche. Whatever this person does to you or anyone else, you have a special love for them. That is to say, you wish them good luck and happiness for the rest of their destiny without qualifications and that doesn't alter it.

         I mean, that is perfectly clear eyed, because love as Aquinas and Christian theological tradition say is exactly the same as knowing the being of the other in its or his isness. You can only do that through love and to know it is to love it, him or her and being in its isness.

It's completely a question between wisdom and love and ignorance. If you don't know what you love, you can't really presume to love it.

Me That's right. I don't think so.

RDL You don't feel proud to belong to them, to be with them or to associate with them? They are cowards?

Me Not necessarily cowards, but if I'm to put in time around someone, in the same space with me...

RDL You've got to feel that they're brave.

Me Very brave.

RDL And you're completely turned off to someone who in your book is a coward?

Me Yes, I don't want any cowards around me. Certainly no cowards. And I don't want any dummies. He has to be very smart also. And I don't want anybody who doesn't enjoy their body.

RDL Etc. etc.

Although I was disappointed at the way things turned out with Laing at this time, I made another trip to his Victorian house in Hampstead, London, this time as his house guest, not Huxley's. If Jutta objected, she did not show it, but remained polite and supportive. In this atmosphere, without the fortress of professional roles, I forgave Laing and opened my heart again.

During this visit, one morning Laing came down the iron spiral staircase, robe-clad and found me at the long wooden kitchen table, sitting over a hot cup of coffee, reading his early publications. He had given me access to the files containing all his published articles. I didn't have far to go since I was sleeping in his office and entertained myself savoring his library. He smiled encouragingly and offered up more of his material.

I was no longer angry at him. Laing had contradicted my repetitive pattern: overcoming his wife's objections privately, instead of expelling me from his familial scene, he had brought me *home* again. I would not choose to be **the other woman** again, but would now find a man of my own. Therein lies the genius of Laing. He knew how to love.

To me his love was expressed more by his actions, by the message conveyed between the words than by anything he said. In spite of all his protestations, his explicit commitment to "whithering away" rather than growing and increasing his options, he had acknowledged me as his partner, shared his real state of being with me, and listened to all of my plans and stories. He had given me the precious gifts of time and attention, and thereby provided me with the motivation to face the ghosts of my past with a renewed spirit. R.D. Laing was my friend.

CHAPTER TWENTY

Epilogue

Our story turned out to be a fairy tale of the real-life variety. Very little turned out as expected. With no time to waste, I forced myself away from discouraging scenarios, no matter how strong the pull. I departed abruptly from some very attractive men when I noticed in their behavior the familiar pattern of covert inaccessibility. I wanted my <u>own</u> man.

Oh, To See Reality

My visit at the Laing household had lasted only a few days. Perhaps it had been more symbolic than substantive. However, the symbolism was powerful: I was not a rejected outcast. Laing had made a stand for me; not the stand I originally had in mind, but a stand nonetheless. Still, in the wake of my disappointment at Laing's not choosing to father a child by me, I had a lot of resorting and adjusting to work through before I could be constructive again. Propelled by that goal, this visit was followed by another visit to the Hampstead home of our friend

Leon Redler. There, from a safe distance, I was resolved to take a closer look at Laing's situation.

Determined to accept reality—whatever that might entail, I would not let go of Laing as he had indelibly requested at our milestone communion on my thirty-ninth birthday. This self-assumed mission had become the core of my sense of purpose. Even if Laing had eventually fallen madly in love with a woman who embodied the combined best features of Simone de Beauvoir and Grace Kelly, I would have overcome my jealousy and learned to accept his chosen woman as well. But the task at hand turned out to be less Herculean in nature. Even in that onerous effort I had a partner.

Jutta had been keeping me informed of Laing's adventures, by telephone, across the Atlantic. And so it was she who told me of Laing's next woman, a London based psychotherapist, Sue. In spite of the fact that Jutta, by then, openly engaged in extramarital relationships, she had a lot to say about Laing's involvement with Sue and I was the perfect audience. I told Laing that I would continue to love him no matter whom he loved or whom he chose as a mate. But when I asked Laing about his involvement with Sue he was not loquacious, and merely managed to tell me that he was spending some time with her.

Even though he was not waxing romantically about her, I wanted to meet Sue. Worse than anything else, I hate being cut off. Although Laing was still primarily based in the living room at his marital home with Jutta, Sue and he went around together. They were an item and if I couldn't have him as my lover and the father of my prospective child, I still did not want to lose him as a loving friend and co-author. Although this pragmatic stance took a lot of working up to and self-talk, it was characteristic of my approach to life. I don't throw away people just because they don't fit the design I might have originally had on them. I have an amazing collection of former lovers enrichingly woven into my life, with their subsequent families and attachments. They are living testaments to the power of flexible thinking. Why throw away love? It's our most precious commodity.

And so I did finally meet Sue: For this encounter, Laing brought her to the house of our friend, Leon, who also lived in Hampstead. I have by now blotted out most of the details—who arrived first, who said what, but I do remember looking at Sue's thighs. She was wearing wildly printed black and white skin-tight capri pants and I kept thinking that she didn't have any fat on them. This is the feature I chose to envy. She seemed delighted to be with Laing and I was intensely aware of her putting her hand on his leg as they sat propped up against some pillows on the floor. On the surface everyone was pleasant and after a couple of hours Laing left with Sue. He seemed comfortable if not captivated, and I wished then that he was leaving with me. In truth, I was happy to get back to compare notes with Jutta.

And The Mills of God Grind Slowly

By 1985, still adjusting to the fact that Laing had decided not to have a baby with me, I started to spend a good deal of time with my friend, Harold Krieger, whom I had known for ten years. He was also going through a difficult adjustment, as well as switching the focus of his attention from a long-term highly successful commercial photography business to our mutual assumption of the management of real estate, which he owned.

Throughout these months of intense comaraderie and openness we grew to love each other. We followed the twenty-two steps delineated herein and embarked on an intimate relationship, showering each other with attention and love. The next time R.D. Laing came back to New York City and called on me for a visit, Harold and I were living together. Ronnie and Harold met and the three of us had a convivial evening together. Laing gave Harold a massage, but refused to continue with our book. Harold sprayed Ronnie's face with moisturizer, synthesizing a London fog and tried to dissuade him from abandoning the book project with me. They seemed to enjoy each other. I wondered what had turned Ronnie away from our long-term endeavor? He, by this time, had a girlfriend of his own (Sue) and a new baby (number 9) called Benjamin, as well. Did he begrudge the fact that I had a new focus of attention in Harold? I didn't think so, because he was happy for me, but I didn't know. Why else would he have dropped the book project just when I was becoming successful? Hadn't he said in the beginning that he was immune to transference? He went off about three in the morning wearing a red rucksack I had given him filled with Harold's face spray and other mementos I cannot remember. I never saw him again, but his Scottish daughter, Fiona, told me that he wore this rucksack some time later on a visit with her in Iona, the beautiful island retreat on the western coast of Scotland.

More than 2 years later, Harold and I had discovered a magnificent old house in the Adirondack mountains where we spent a good deal of time together, relating, liquidating our separate businesses and taking care of our New York City real estate which was now supporting us both. We had married and planned to have a baby, but with none forthcoming, we focused our nurturing attention, instead, on each other, our friends and our over-attended, Samoyed, Doginie. When I realized that I was not likely to have a baby, I started readdressing myself to the manuscript for the book with Laing, *How to Take Your Own Advice*, which was the working title then. It had evolved into my version of what happened between Laing and myself. It was a love story. It was a love story with a good ending. Because Laing had honored me and taken me home again after our having been together, I had honored myself, by being with Harold.

I sent the manuscript to Laing. He celebrated it. After reading it, he called me twenty times from Kitzbuhel, Austria, in the Alps, where he was then living with Margeurita (who had been his secretary since 1980), and their baby, Charles. Laing called to encourage me. He edited some of the revised manuscript and told me to get it to a publisher. He thought it was ready and that many women would identify with me. He said that the book had taken 9 years to create, a long gestation period, and that I should stop showing it to friends and get it published. I was thrilled with his renewed enthusiasm and clarity. He completely stopped drinking for the last year of his life. We spoke on the phone regularly during his last year. He always seemed available and receptive and intense. He called me in Lake Placid and said that he wanted to visit Harold and me with Marguerita and Charles.

He edited my work and wrote more of his own. After I calmed down from my initial thrill at his eagerness to go on with the book after all, I decided not to go on with this project myself, because I felt that Laing was not promoting himself as an example of the result I wanted our readers to achieve. He had said repeatedly that he didn't want to change, but the book was about transformation. Also I imagined that I would have to cater to his sensibilities when telling our tale to the point of making our story completely myopic. He tried to convince me to prevail, but he listened to my objections.

About two weeks before he died, he advised me to sit down with Harold for a few hours and discuss the possibility of finishing this book without any further results from him. I, in turn, advised him to sit down with Margeurita for a few hours and discuss the possibility of finishing this book with a further result from him. He said I was being impertinent. I said my suggestion was a gift to him. He said that he would think about it.

During this long and solemn conversation I told him that he was part of my identity, that I would always love him. I told him that I could not ever walk away from him without offering an opening, an opportunity and without offering him a confrontation, as I was doing just then. He said he loved me. I felt very close to him, once again, as if there was no barrier between us, as if we were different parts of one entity. Nevertheless, I told him that I hoped he would not abandon me. True to form, he said that if I didn't hear from him right away, that did not mean he was not thinking of me. Actually we were saying goodbye.

When I referred to my reservations about pandering to his sensibilities in telling our story as inhibiting, he said, emphatically, "Write it when I'm dead, but *write* it!"

I didn't know he was going to die soon, but he did. He had had 2 heart attacks in the past 2 years. His reference to death and the gravity of his tone evoked the presence of a strange, but familiar shadow. He had never focused on his death with me. I did not know about the heart attacks. He died playing tennis in St. Tropez on August 23, 1989.

It doesn't exactly feel like he's dead now, more like he has changed form, into pure energy. I can still see him and hear his voice inside me. Some mornings in New York City, I run along the river, playing the tapes of our conversations together, laughing and crying as I go along.

CHAPTER TWENTY-ONE

Appendix

What Works in Psychotherapy: A Report

"Every method and school of psychotherapy is actually a system of applied ethics couched in the idiom of treatment, and each reflects the personality, values and aspirations of its founder."

Thomas Szasz

"The cure of the soul has to be effected by the use of certain charms, and these charms are fair words."

Socrates

A review of the psychotherapy research results led me to believe that psychotherapists of different disciplines were much more alike than they professed to be, but my interviews with selected professionals convincingly confirmed this belief. The principle of Occam's razor says that the simplest, most encompassing explanation is best. This is what I was looking for.

A leading behavioristic therapist and author, Arnold Lazarus, Ph.D., in answer to my question, "What makes people grow?" suggested that the active ingredients in therapy were performance-based measures. He said it was the doing of new and desired behaviors that insured the client's therapeutic progress. He felt that insight-based therapies are often useless.

I asked him, in good faith, if he was so powerful a person (perhaps his reputation preceded him) that clients just walked in, he then analyzed their difficulties and gave them appropriate, homework assignments and off they went?

He replied that some of his patients take a year of corrective emotional experience before they try any new performance-based measures.

Might this delay period, before the client is ready to go out and practice new behaviors, be what the Freudians refer to as resistance and transference phenomena? Dr. Lazarus would prefer not to be thought of as a "closet analyst." He thought resistance might have something to do with this phenomenon, however.

Irving Weinstein, Ph.D. is a New York based, self-described, post Freudian/eclectic psychologist who had been practicing for over twenty years at the time that I interviewed him for the *Report On Effective Psychotherapy: Legislative Testimony*, 1981. Queried about how therapy works, he described it as a reparenting procedure. Although the issues of performance-based measures, which were so central to Lazarus' concept of therapy, were never raised, Dr. Weinstein recalled many instances when he had given clients homework assignments until the desired behavior was approximated.

According to Andrew Collier's memory of a lecture given by Laing, as he reports in *R.D. Laing: The Philosophy and Politics of Psychotherapy* (1977), Laing replied in the following manner when asked what the differences of method were between the various schools of analytical psychotherapy - Freudian, Kleinian etc.:

"There are no differences of method, only of terminology; for instance, in the course of an analysis by a Kleinian, the word 'breast' might be used a hundred times more than in an orthodox Freudian analysis, while the orthodox Freudian would use the word 'penis' and 'vagina' a hundred times more. Laing was then asked what words he would use more than other analysts, and he said he would be inclined to use the same words as the other person (who was being analyzed)."

Hans Strupp, a leading researcher in psychotherapy, feels that growth is promoted by non-specific factors such as understanding, trust and warmth which are not the exclusive province of any single therapeutic school of thought. By and large he feels that all prominent therapeutic approaches have been shown to be equally effective. "The art of psychotherapy may consist largely of judicious and sensitive applications of a given technique, delicate decisions on when to press a point or when to be patient, when to be warm and understanding, or when to be remote. The therapist structures the situation in bold relief so that the patient is forced to renounce the helping relationship or undergo change." (Gurman & Razin, 1978). When Strupp compared groups of depressed male college students, some of them treated by professionally credentialed and experienced psychotherapists and others treated by benign college professors whose training was not in psychotherapy, on the average the results were the same! This startling conclusion remained true even after a one year follow-up. The experimenters concluded that positive change was generally attributable to the healing effects of a benign human relationship.

"...there is no self; there is no transmigration of a self; but there are deeds and the continued effect of deeds."

Buddhist philosopher

Who was R.D. Laing?

Laing, R(onald) D(avid), British psychiatrist (b. Oct. 7, 1927, Glasgow, Scotland—d. Aug. 23, 1989, St. Tropez, France), polarized the mental health community with his first book, *The Divided Self* (1960), in which he theorized that schizophrenia might be a rational defensive reaction to unbearable pressures from family members and inappropriate psychiatric treatment. Laing rejected the prevailing theory that the symptoms characteristic of schizophrenia arose from genetic or biochemical causes and denounced the use of drugs, lobotomies and electroshock therapy, then commonly prescribed for schizophrenics. After graduating (1951) in medicine from the University of Glasgow, Laing served (1951-53) as a British army psychiatrist. He taught (1953-56) at the University of Glasgow, trained in psychoanalysis, and conducted research (1956-60) at the Tavistock Clinic in London. He then put his unorthodox theories into practice as an associate of the Tavistock Institute (1960-89), director of the Langham Clinic (1962-65), chairman of the Philadelphia Association (1964-82), and founding director of Kingsley Hall, an experimental community house in London. Laing's approach to madness as a form of individual free expression, combined with a series of well-publicized experiments in the therapeutic use of mescaline and LSD, earned him cult status in the antipsychiatry movement of the 1960s. He modified his theories somewhat in his later books, which included *Sanity, Madness and the Family* (1965), *The Politics of Experience* (1967), *The Politics of the Family* (1971), and the autobiographical *Wisdom, Madness and Folly: The Making of a Psychiatrist* (1985).

Taken from: *1990 Britannica Book of the Year*, Encyclopaedia Britannica, Inc.

Who Is Roberta Russell?

Roberta Russell was born January 28, 1944 in New York City. She received her BA in psychology from Queens College in 1964 and did graduate work at the University of Oklahoma and CUNY and then went on to become a computer systems analyst. From 1970 to 1988 she founded and ran R.R. Latin Associates, Inc., an exclusive professional search firm serving the computer industry. She has also conducted workshops on Self Marketing at the Yale School of Business and has been invited to speak on the subject at New York University and The New School.

Russell has been affiliated with the National Accreditation Association and American Examining Board of Psychoanalysis, Inc., Education and Accreditation Committees as an elected public member and in 1981 published *Report on Effective Psychotherapy: Legislative Testimony.* She was invited to speak on her findings at Yale and at conferences in Europe as well as in the U.S. In 1980 she met R.D. Laing and a year later embarked with him on *"R.D. Laing & Me: Lessons in Love,"* an innovative project which drew on her work in the fields of psychotherapy and self-marketing. She resides in New York City and Lake Placid with her husband, Harold Krieger, and is currently implementing *R.D. Laing & Me: Lessons in Love* in her own life.

Recommended Reading

The Reign of Error: Psychiatry, Authority and Law
Lee Coleman, M.D.
Boston: Beacon Press, 1984
(An exploration into psychiatric authority.)

Principles of Intensive Psychotherapy
Frieda Fromm-Reichmann, M.D.
Chicago: University of Chicago Press, 1950
(A primer of psychotherapeutic technique.)

Handbook of Psychotherapy and Behavior Change
editors: Sol L. Garfield and Allen E. Bergin
New York: John Wiley & Sons, 1978, 1986
(A comprehensive analysis and report of the research developments into psychotherapy.)

Vital Lies, Simple Truths
Daniel Goleman
New York: Simon & Schuster, 1985
(An examination of the psychology of self-deception.)

Cure or Heal?
A Study of Therapeutic Experience
E. Graham Howe, M.D.
London: George Allen & Unwin Ltd., 1965
(An existential and spiritual study of problems in communication and relationship.)

The Politics of Experience
R.D. Laing, M.D.
New York: Pantheon, 1967
(A classic experiment in undoing the alienation this book attempts to document.)

Sonnets
R.D. Laing, M.D.
New York: Pantheon, 1979, 1980
(A poetic examination of the predicaments and contradictions of human nature.)

On Caring
Milton Mayeroff
New York: Perennial Library, Harper & Row, 1971
(A manual of caring and being cared for.)

Community Mental Health Principles & Practice
Loren R. Mosher, M.D. & Lorenzo Burti, M.D.
New York, London: W.W. Norton & Company, 1989
(The what & how of effective community mental health practice.)

The Healing Journey
Claudio Naranjo, M.D.
New York: Pantheon Books, 1971
(A discussion of the psychotherapeutic use of drugs by those
sympathetic to their nature.)

Report on Effective Psychotherapy: Legislative Testimony
Roberta Russell
New York: R.R. Latin Associates, Inc., 1981 (now available through
Hillgarth Press)
(A documented and anecdotal report and analysis of the active
ingredients in psychotherapy.)

The Myth of Psychotherapy
Thomas Szasz, M.D.
Garden City, N.Y.: Anchor Press, Doubleday, 1979
(An examination of the rhetoric of psychotherapy.)

Fragments of an Analysis with Freud
Joseph Wortis
New York, London: Jason Aaronson, 1984
(A vivid account of an analysis of Wortis by Freud.)

Sayings of Buddha
Mt. Vernon, N.Y.: Peter Pauper Press, 1957
(One of many excellent books on Buddhism.)